# A GOOD FINANCIAL ADVISOR WILL TELL YOU...

EVERYTHING YOU NEED TO KNOW ABOUT RETIREMENT,
GENERATING LIFETIME INCOME, AND PLANNING YOUR LEGACY

AVIVA
PUBLISHING
NEW YORK

**ROBERT J. LUNA, CIMA® &
JEREMY A. KISNER, CFP®**

**A Good Financial Advisor Will Tell You...**
Everything You Need to Know about Retirement,
Generating Lifetime Income, and Planning Your Legacy
Copyright © 2012 by Robert J. Luna, CIMA® & Jeremy A. Kisner, CFP®

**Address all inquiries to:**
SureVest Capital Management
C/O Jeremy Kisner
2201 East Camelback Road, Ste 315B, Phoenix, AZ 85016
*ph* 877-975-7400
www.Good-Financial-Advisor.com

**Published by:**
Aviva Publishing
Lake Placid, NY
518-523-1320
www.avivapubs.com

ISBN: 978-1-935586-49-4

Library of Congress Control Number: 2011941524

**Editor:** Tyler Tichelaar
**Cover Design:** Christine Ashton
**Interior Layout:** Fusion Creative Works, www.fusioncw.com

Every attempt has been made to properly source all quotes.

Printed in the United States of America

First Edition

# DEDICATION

---

This book is written for and dedicated to our clients. We can never adequately express how much we appreciate your business and your friendship. It is because of you that we are able to support our families and make a good living doing exactly what we love. Your stories and your wisdom have enriched our lives. Although these two words seem so inadequate, we simply want to say—Thank You!

# ACKNOWLEDGMENTS

We started out in this business when we were very young. We did not have any clients or a great deal of wisdom or insight. Today, we manage millions of dollars for hundreds of families and business owners all across the country. That would never have been possible without the support of some very important people.

First, we want to thank our spouses, both of whom were working with us side-by-side in the early years of the business. As our business and families grew, they were promoted to the more important (and challenging) job—"stay at home moms." Through the years, their support has been unconditional. They put up with long work hours and incessant talk about economic matters. We are both fortunate to have what every man wants in a spouse: an equal partner.

Secondly, we want to thank our team. Nothing is better than coming to work each day and being surrounded by hard-working, competent people who truly care about what they do. Our goal has never been to build the biggest investment advisory business. We simply wanted to work with a small team of "all-stars" and build a business that would make us proud. Thank you for making that dream a reality.

Lastly, we want to thank our children: Chloe, Gracie, Maya, and Bella, for providing a constant source of love, inspiration, and laughter.

# CONTENTS

# INTRODUCTION

---

*"The art is not in making money, but in keeping it."*
— Proverb

Let's start with what this book is not. This book is not an "introduction to investing" book. Millions of those are out there, and they typically put people to sleep. Therefore, this book is *not* going to explain: What is a stock? What is a mutual fund? How do you create a family budget? Yada, yada, yada. This book was written for the millions of people who could be called the "mass affluent"—those hardworking, successful individuals and families who have managed to accumulate $500,000 to $10,000,000, and those who are focused upon working toward that kind of affluence. Through meetings with hundreds of current and prospective clients, we have seen how people accumulate small fortunes, and then frequently lose a good portion of them through bad investments and poor planning.

Many people acquire their fortunes through systematic saving in qualified retirement plans (i.e. pensions, 401k, etc.), through real estate, the sale of a small business, or an inheritance. Each of these methods of acquiring wealth is very legitimate, but none of them involve active management of your investments. The accumulation stage (birth through the end of your career) of your financial life is much simpler and more forgiving than the strategy required for the distribution and legacy planning stage that occurs during your retirement years.

Once people retire, they frequently roll over retirement accounts that were administered by their employer to an IRA where they have full control. They also sell businesses or real estate and have a lump sum of money to invest. Most people have never been in the position to invest in this way before, or at least not at this level, and not when the stakes are so high. In fact, most people's largest assets (in order) are their home, their company retirement plan, and then cash value life insurance. What do those three assets have in common? You typically don't look at their value every day, and they are not considered liquid by most of their owners.

What many people fail to realize when they retire is that they have just employed themselves to become the pension fund manager for themselves and their family's future. What that means is they may no longer have the luxury of not needing to take income from their investments. When you are in this situation, your investment portfolio has in essence become your employer. The performance of your portfolio will now dictate in large part the lifestyle that you and your family can enjoy in the future. If your portfolio does not generate enough income, you no longer have the option of just working more hours or taking on a side project. Your portfolio is more important now than ever, as are other financial decisions you will be making. You have entered the major leagues of investing and you are up to bat. The questions you now need to ask are:

- How should I change my investment mix?

- How much can I afford to take from my account on a monthly or annual basis?

- From which investments should I take the money?

Professional pension fund managers face these questions each day. You now have a decision to make—you can either answer these questions for yourself, or you can hire a professional to answer them for you. It's a tough decision whether to manage your investments yourself or to hire a professional. If you are considering doing it yourself, you should be aware of some of the mistakes we frequently see among do-it-yourself-ers.

Once people have control and liquidity, they begin to exhibit what we call "Retail Investor Behavior." As you may have guessed, this behavior is not a good thing. Retail Investor Behavior can best be demonstrated by looking at a study by Dalbar Inc., a leading investment research firm. Its study of investor behavior found that although the U.S. stock market (as measured by the S&P 500 index) grew at an average annualized rate of 9.14% between 1990 and 2010, the average investor in the stock market only earned 3.83%. The same was true for investors in bonds. The Barclay's Aggregate Bond Index earned 6.89% over the same 20 year period. The average investor in bonds only realized 1.01%. That is stunning! Retail investors are earning less than half the market's return. Why is that? The investments work. The problem is investor behavior. However, before you can successfully analyze any investment or financial plan, it is imperative first to understand the psychological biases that prevent most people from succeeding at managing their own money.

The investing failures are not due to people being stupid. The majority of people we meet and work with are quite bright. Many of our clients are Ph.D.'s, engineers, lawyers, CPA's, successful business owners and college professors. The reason why most people make poor investors is that they are human. Human beings are hard-wired to make decisions with their hearts and justify them with logic. Greed and fear rule the day. Unfortunately, the fear and adrenaline that kept humans alive when we lived in the jungle does not serve us well as modern day investors.

This book is going to explain some of the most common ways people destroy themselves (financially). We will also delve into the new and fascinating field of behavioral finance. In other words, we are not just going to list typical mistakes investors make. Rather, we are going to explain WHY people make the same mistakes over and over again. Then we will give you examples of what you can do differently so your investments remain safe and continue to grow.

Take a moment to reflect on these questions:

- Are you overwhelmed by the number and complexity of investment choices?

- Have you ever wondered why investments always seem to go down after you buy them?

- Do you always feel like you are in a reactionary mode to investing?

- Are you unsure how to find a financial advisor you can trust?

- If you hire a financial advisor, how do you evaluate his or her performance?

When you finish reading this book, you will have the answers to these and many other questions. You will be a more educated investor and a better consumer of financial services. This book will dispel many of the most dangerous myths and misconceptions about money. More importantly, this book is going to provide insights to help you become financially successful during the second half of your life. You do not have to be the typical retail investor. There is a better way, and we will explain it in terms you can understand. As Einstein said, "You should make things as simple as possible, but no simpler."

Let's conclude this introduction with a few thoughts about what it means to be financially successful. It has nothing to do with your current income or this quarter's return on your portfolio. Financial success means that you can afford to live an extraordinary life and a life that you love. Financial success means that you will always be able to afford your current lifestyle. More importantly, it means that you have the financial security to live your life without financial stress. As Jerry Maguire said in the movie named for him, "I wish you my kind of happiness."

Jeremy A. Kisner, CFP®

Robert J. Luna, CIMA®

December 1, 2011

# CHAPTER 1

# THE PSYCHOLOGY OF INVESTING

*"Good judgment comes from experience and experience....*
*Well, that comes from poor judgment."*
— A.A. Milne

This first chapter will explain many of the natural human instincts and behaviors as they relate to investing. The first step in making better decisions is to understand how you are influenced and how your brain comes to certain conclusions. The remaining chapters will provide information and  insights on financial issues in the context of what you have learned in the first part of this book. We will cover the most important issues related to retirement, income planning, and legacy planning, as well as the most common myths, misconceptions, and "stupid" ideas that we see in our roles as financial advisors and professional money managers.

Financial professionals frequently base their decisions, advice, and teachings on academic models such as Modern Portfolio Theory,

Efficient Market Hypothesis, Capital Asset Pricing Model, Technical Analysis, and others. These are simply theories that economists use to predict how people are going to act and how investments are going to be valued in a free market. The problem with applying these theories to real life is that they assume individuals make rational and unbiased decisions in order to maximize their own benefits. In fact, that assumption is the basis for the entire field of economics. However, it is clear to those who actually work with individual investors that these assumptions are not reliable. People frequently act irrationally. The funny thing is that investors can recognize the irrationality in others but rarely in themselves. Dan Ariely wrote a good book on this topic—the *New York Times* bestseller *Predictably Irrational*.

Today, we have far more information bombarding us at all times than we are able to process. This situation has become more pronounced with the rise of the Internet and the 24-hour news cycle with streaming headlines, alerts, and breaking news. As information comes into our brain, it first affects the portion of our brain that controls feelings and emotions (the limbic system, and more specifically the amygdala). This part of the brain makes the vast majority of our judgments and decisions because it can process information relatively quickly and easily.

Making decisions based on deductive, logical reasoning is much more laborious and time-consuming because that part of our brain (the neo-cortex) can only handle one step at a time. For that reason, we love to use computers to do our linear thinking for us (thank you Microsoft Excel). However, it is important to understand that in addition to being faster than the human brain for many functions, computers do not take shortcuts or impute emotion, mood, or past experience into their analysis. This result can be both good and bad. You need both rational decision-making and human elements to be a successful investor.

The rational and emotional parts of our brains are in constant contact with each other and influence each other. However, the default mechanism for decision-making (which, therefore, makes the lion's share of decisions) is the emotional/intuitive part of our brain. Unfortunately, a lot of good investing practices are counterintuitive. The old adage is that fear and greed are what move investors and markets. That is largely true, but it's a bit of an over-simplification. Let's look at some of the specific biases we see with investors.

## MENTAL SHORTCUTS

*"The only reason a great many American families don't own an elephant is that they have never been offered an elephant for a dollar down and easy weekly payments."*
— Mad Magazine

Behavioral finance is a relatively new area of study that explores the intersection of psychology and applied economics. The field of behavioral finance really gained credibility and acceptance in 2002 when the Nobel Prize in Economics was awarded to psychologist Daniel Kahneman and economist Vernon Smith.[1] They demonstrated, through a series of studies, that most people are incapable of analyzing complex decisions, especially if the consequences of those decisions are uncertain. Furthermore, people are more likely to

---

1    Source: Klein, Gary. *Sources of Power: How People Make Decisions.* Cambridge, MA: MIT Press, 1999.

rely on intuition and feelings as the basis for their decisions when information is incomplete or the goals are ill-defined or competing, and the decision relies on interaction with others. Many, if not all, of these factors come into play when trying to analyze investments and develop financial plans. In other words, people rely on their feelings when making financial decisions because using logic is too complex.

The brain's tendency to seek out mental shortcuts is what leads people to gravitate toward rules that are simplistic and easy to remember. Even some financial advisors fall into these traps and preach them as gospel. Some of our favorite examples are:

- The rule of 100 (your allocation to stocks should be your age minus 100)

- Buy stocks with low price earnings ratios (P/E)

- Sell in May and go away (summer months are bad for stocks)

- Dogs of the Dow (buy the 10 Dow stocks with the highest dividend yield), and

- My favorite of all, the Super Bowl Indicator (if the NFC team wins the Super Bowl then we are headed for a good year in the stock market. If the AFC team wins, however, watch out below!)

Some of these "rules" may sound silly, but many people put stock in these ideas. Wouldn't it be great if it were just that easy?

Let's try to get a better understanding of how mental shortcuts work. We know that our brain uses shortcuts to reduce the complexity of decisions and enable us to come up with answers without fully digesting all of the available information. A common example is assuming that two things that share similar qualities are alike. This bias is known as: **Representativeness**. Consider the following example:

Mary is quiet, studious and concerned with social issues. While an undergraduate at Berkeley, she majored in English literature and environmental studies. Given this information, indicate which of the following three choices is most probable:

A. Mary is a librarian

B. Mary is a librarian and a member of the Sierra Club

C. Mary works for the banking industry[2]

This question was posed to undergraduate investment students, MBA candidates, and financial advisors. In all three groups, more than half of the subjects chose "B." People selected answer B because being a librarian and a member of the Sierra Club is representative of someone who is studious and concerned with social issues. However, the question asked which choice is most probable?

Choice A (being a librarian) is always more probable than choice B (being a librarian *and* a member of the Sierra Club) since A is a subset of B. Typically, a quarter to a third of those surveyed understood this and selected the answer "A." However, the best choice is "C" (Mary works in the banking industry). Why? It is because so many more jobs exist in the banking industry than in libraries. Based on the sheer number of positions in each industry, it is much more probable that Mary works in banking. Very few people pick "C" as

2   Adapted from: Nofsinger, John. *The Psychology of Investing*. 4th ed. Upper Saddle River, NJ: Prentice-Hall, 2010.

their answer because working in banking is not "representative" of the facts presented. This example reflects how a mental shortcut may lead you astray.

## Good Companies vs. Good Investments

A common mental shortcut that investors take is to assume that a good company is the same thing as a good investment. Good companies are typically characterized as those that have consistently grown their sales and earnings and have well-respected products or services. Frequently, those companies are very popular investments and may be overvalued. These companies are typically known as "growth" companies (i.e. Google or Facebook). Growth companies are frequently fully valued or overvalued and likely to take a hit the first time they miss an earnings target. In other words, at some point, they cannot continue to meet expectations. Many times, the best investments are companies that have recently had a misstep and their value has already declined. The best investments may also be companies in a sector of the economy that is out of favor at the moment, such as an energy company during a recession when demand for energy is lower. These out-of-favor companies are typically a bit cheaper and are known as "value" investments. Over long periods of time, value stocks have had better risk-adjusted returns than growth stocks. **Risk-adjusted returns** is an important concept we will refer to throughout this book. It simply means how much return you are getting for the level of risk you are taking.

**What have you done for me lately?**

Perhaps the most common mental shortcut we see is called **Recency Bias**. In short, you may feel that recent past performance (good or bad) will continue. The human mind is wired to see the world linearly. We seek out patterns even when none exist. We convince ourselves that whatever is the most recent pattern will continue indefinitely—even in the face of overwhelming evidence that it won't. The result is an ongoing cycle of booms and busts.

The media tends to feed our recency bias by focusing on recent performance and spotlighting the biggest winners and losers of the day, week, month, or year. You always have to keep in mind that the media is in the business of selling advertising, not making you a better investor. If the media were interested in making you a better investor, it might talk about topics such as **Reversion to the Mean**.

Reversion to the Mean simply means that investment valuations tend to return to their long-term averages. For example, residential real estate has consistently been valued at 3.0 times the median household income. From 1980 to 1999, the valuations for residential real estate nationwide were consistently between 2.9 and 3.1 times the median household income. Home prices started to skyrocket in 2000. Homes were valued at an average of 4.0 times the median income by 2004 and 4.6 times the median income at the peak in 2006.[3] Most people then extrapolated this trend, expecting it to continue. They figured home prices would continue to rise and were soon going to be 5.0 times the median income and then 6.0 times. What actually happened is the bubble burst, so home prices have declined for the

---

3    Source: Harvard University, Joint Center for Housing Studies, *State of the Nation's Housing*, 2007.

past five years. Today, home prices are currently getting closer to their long-term historical average of 3.0 times median income.

Most investment professionals, along with evidence from hundreds of years of history, will tell you that you have a bubble when valuations diverge significantly from their long-term averages (the mean). Long-term averages are made up of periods of overvaluation and periods of undervaluation. Therefore, if you want to know whether a price trend is likely to continue, you ought to look at it in terms of the relationship of current prices to long-term historical averages. That being said, always remember that just because something is cheap does not mean that it can't get cheaper, and just because something is overvalued does not mean that it cannot become more overvalued. The key is to manage risk. You have much more risk when buying an asset that is already well above its historical long-term valuation.

## EMOTIONS AND INVESTMENT DECISIONS

*"All I ask is for the chance to prove that money*
*can't make me happy."*
— Bill Vaughn

Emotions affect almost all of our decisions. Why would something as fickle as your "mood" have a large impact on your long-term financial decisions? Most likely because your investment decisions are based on your expectations for the future. You are expecting the company in which you invest to grow and prosper. You are expecting that other people will want to live/work/shop in the same area where you buy a piece of real estate. When you are in a good mood, you genuinely believe that everything you want to happen in the future is more likely to occur. It has also been proven that when people are sad or depressed, they are less likely to buy big ticket items or make long-term investments.

Did you know that studies reflect that when the sun is shining, people are in a better mood? So, how does sunshine affect people's financial decisions? According to the *Journal of Applied Science*, studies show that people leave bigger tips for waiters when the weather is good. You must be thinking that we are talking about people who were sitting at an outdoor cafe enjoying the good weather. We're not. Good weather makes people happier even if they are not outside enjoying the good weather. Another thing that affects people's mood is music. High-end retailers play upbeat music in their stores because it has been proven that people who are in a good mood spend more. The better your mood, the more likely you are to take on riskier investments.[4]

Emotional decision-making is one of the reasons why retail investors in the stock market underperform market indexes. Retail investors "buy high and sell low," which is obviously the opposite of what they intend. They "buy high" because they are feeling the most optimistic, and therefore, they are willing to take more risk after recent success (near market peaks). Investors are the least optimistic after recent losses (market declines) so they are less willing to accept risk. That is why they sell at (or near) market lows.

Women will tell us men that we need to be more emotional, which is probably true (actually, when our wives tell us so, it must be true). However, when it comes to investing, we encourage you to try to be less emotional, or at least to hire someone who can be less emotional

---

4    Source: Rind, Bruce. "Effects of Beliefs about Weather Conditions on Tipping." *Journal of Applied Social Psychology* 26 (1996): 137-147.

about your investment decisions. The financial professional's role is to help you keep perspective by minimizing the influence of your current emotional state and recent experiences upon your investments so you can focus more on your long-term goals.

If you are managing your own money, follow this simple advice: Do not take more risk after seeing gains and do not reduce your risk after taking losses. As tempting as that may be, it usually pays to do the opposite.

## OVERCONFIDENCE

We just showed that emotion is not your friend when it comes to investing. So let us ask you this: Who is generally considered more emotional, men or women? Most people would say that women are considered more emotional than men. You would then deduce that women are worse investors than men (a perfect example of a mental shortcut and representativeness). However, you would be wrong. Why? Emotion is just one of the psychological biases that gets investors in trouble. Another problem we see is **overconfidence**, which is more prevalent in men.

Many of the investors we meet are overconfident—something easy to see based both on statements we hear them say as well as their actions. We always say in our business that the worst thing that can happen to an investor is to have a good run early because success amplifies overconfidence and feeds **self-attribution** bias. Self-attribution bias means that when a decision turns out well, it is attributed to that person's skill. However, if the decision turns out poorly, then results are attributed to bad luck or other factors. Inevitably, success leads to misplaced confidence in one's abilities to pick investments, which leads to more risk taking and more frequent trading.

## Worst Case Scenario

When I (Robert Luna) was working as a risk analyst for a Wall Street firm, I had a retail client (let's call him Mr. Jones) who came into one of our retail branches. He wanted to open up a margin account that he would be using for "swing and day-trading," meaning he would be buying and selling stocks on a short-term basis with the intent to turn fast profits. When reviewing his account, I noticed his occupation was listed as "trader." This job description concerned me because it meant that his livelihood was based on his ability to pull enough money out of his account on a monthly basis to pay his bills. The reality was his withdrawal rate of 14% was unsustainable based on any measure. I just hoped for his sake that "this time it was different."

According to the broker who opened his account, our client had sold his family business for $250,000 a year earlier and parlayed that into roughly $1.4 million. He had achieved this wealth by day-trading stocks such as CMGI, LYCOS, E-Trade, JDSU and other Internet high flyers. It was late 1999, and fortunes were being made. Our local branch was very impressed by this guy, but it was my responsibility to protect our firm's money. I had a sinking feeling in my stomach when I heard the "good news" about his abilities. I knew the level of risk he was taking was astronomical. Everyone else was blinded by the results.

Within one week, Mr. Jones' account popped up on my screen. It is not a good thing when your account pops up on the risk analyst's screen. Mr. Jones had fully margined his portfolio, meaning that his $1.4 million account was now holding $2.8 million in stock. That meant that he had $1.4 million of his own money and was borrowing the other $1.4 million from our firm at the maximum amount of leverage allowed (50% equity). If his stocks declined at all, he would be notified either to deposit more funds into his account or sell some stock to bring his account back to 50% equity.

Within a day, I was on the phone to Mr. Jones. He still had the same $1.4 million dollar margin loan, but his equity (the brokerage firm's collateral) had fallen to $1.35 million, meaning he had lost $50,000 the previous day. The call went something like: "Mr. Jones, you have a margin call. You either need to deposit $50,000 into your account by the end of the day or sell $100,000 in stock." Mr. Jones replied, "No problem," and took care of our margin call by selling stock. For those of you who remember this period in market history, tech stocks were very volatile. When I say "volatile," that is code for going down in flames.

My company and I continued this daily rapport with Mr. Jones over the next month. Each time he met his margin call by selling stock instead of depositing new funds. As mentioned, his occupation was "trader" and his family business had been sold to fund this new venture. So, if he needed to pay for something, the funds had to come out of his portfolio, which at the moment was hemorrhaging cash. His only option to meet our requirements was to sell more stock. Each time, Mr. Jones sold only enough to meet our minimum requirements.

This cat and mouse game continued until October 1999. The stock market storm started to intensify, and what had been tropical turned into a full-blown hurricane. We witnessed the sell-off pick up steam and many stocks started falling between 5-10% daily. I watched his account go from $1.3 million a month earlier to $425,000, and he was still fully leveraged, meaning he owed $212,000 against the stock.

I wish this story had a happy ending. This man, who was extremely confident in his abilities to trade the markets, resorted to becoming a buy-and-hold long-term investor, meaning the stock he intended to sell a day later when it was up 10% had turned against him so fast that he became paralyzed. I have seen this situation happen time and time again over my career when stocks move against investors. Mr. Jones resorted to Internet chat boards, grasping for any positive story that would justify holding onto his losing positions. He was very emotional every time I spoke with him, and he literally came to tears on several occasions. He promised daily to make sales by the end of the day, but ultimately, at the bitter end, my company was forced to do the liquidations for him because he just couldn't bring himself to sell.

In the end over a four day period in mid-October, the decline worsened to the point where even my company couldn't reduce his margin position quickly enough. This man who sold his thirty-year-old family business to become a stock trader, and just months earlier had $1.4 million in his account, was about to receive a call he never envisioned. "Mr. Jones, I am sorry to inform you that we needed to liquidate your entire account today. Unfortunately, the market moved against you so quickly that even after selling all of your remaining positions, we couldn't completely cover your margin balance. We will need you to deposit $16,000 to make good on the money you borrowed from our firm."

I saw one situation after another where people lost money they could not afford to lose. This scenario, unfortunately, was the story of my career for two long years as a risk analyst. However, these stories and experiences shaped my philosophy of wealth protection and risk-management. The truth is that the most difficult part of investing your own money is separating emotion from the investment process and knowing your limitations. In practice, very few individuals can truly do that.

## Better than Average?

One aspect of overconfidence is the inherent human quality that most people believe they are better than average at most things. For example, in one study a large group of college students were asked to rate their driving abilities. If people were to perceive themselves accurately, one-third of the group should have rated themselves as average drivers, one-third as below average, and one-third above average. However, 82% rated themselves above average. Clearly, some of those surveyed were overconfident in their driving abilities. This same overconfidence phenomenon can be seen in many areas of society. The average person thinks that other people are more likely than him- or herself to be in a car accident, get a divorce, get fired from a job, etc. Smokers think they will not get lung cancer even though they know that smoking causes cancer.[5]

---

5    Source: Svenson, Ola. "Are We All Less Risky and More Skillful Than Our Fellow Drivers?" *Acta Psychologica* 47 (1981): 143-148.

Another aspect of overconfidence is the "illusion of control." You may feel you have more control over the outcome of a situation if you are involved in the process or if you are given a choice. For example, most people will bet more on a coin toss if they can place their bet before the coin is tossed. People also believe they have a higher probability of winning the lottery if they get to pick their numbers. These are good examples of a process where your involvement may make you feel better about your probability of success. The reality is that your involvement has no statistical impact on the outcome.

The advent of online trading has enabled investors to have more involvement in the investment process than ever before. This involvement has led to an increase in the "illusion of control" and a greater degree of overconfidence. People who trade their own stocks online typically have higher turnover (i.e. more frequent buying and selling) than those working through a financial advisor or placing their trades over the phone. Higher turnover is correlated with lower investment performance. The most overconfident investors in a study[6] were single men, followed by married men, then married women, and finally, single women. Single men had the highest turnover and lowest net investment returns. Single women were the least overconfident, traded less frequently, and had the highest net investment returns.

The problem with overconfidence is that it causes you to take more risk. The increase in risk has two aspects:

6    Source: Barber, Barb and Terrance Odean. "Trading is Hazardous to your Wealth: The Common Stock Performance of Individual Investors." *Journal of Finance* 55 (2000): 773-806.

1. <u>More speculative investments</u>: Overconfident investors are less likely to invest in those old stodgy blue chip companies with strong balance sheets and good dividends. Instead, they are more likely to invest in smaller start-up companies. They think they know which company is going to become the next Google, Facebook, or biotech company that is going to change the world. In other words, they are looking to hit home runs instead of singles.

2. <u>Lack of diversification</u>: Overconfident investors make bigger bets on fewer investments (aka "concentrated positions"). They are more likely to speculate with a large percentage of their portfolio on precious metals like gold or silver. In our investment advisory business, we make a lot of well-researched, well-diversified, small investments, and then we monitor them all day, every day. We typically do not invest more than 2% of a client's portfolio in any one stock or more than 4% in any single bond. However, it is not uncommon when we first see a prospective client's portfolio to find the person has 10-20% of his or her portfolio in a single stock or bond. You should always remember that no matter how much you love a company or believe in its future, anything can happen. Just think of all the companies that investors thought couldn't fail: Enron, WorldCom, Lucent, CMGI, General Motors, Chrysler, Washington Mutual...to name a few. Many other big, well-established companies didn't fail but lost 50-90% of their value from 2007-2009 (e.g. Bank of America, Citibank, GE, AIG).

## YOUR RISK TOLERANCE AND THE CASINO EFFECT

*"If only God gave me a clear sign, like making a large deposit in my name at a Swiss bank."*
— Woody Allen

In developing any financial plan, it's vital to consider your risk tolerance. Most financial advisors will ask you a series of questions to determine how much risk you want to take. What you may not realize is how fickle your risk tolerance is. The best scenario is that your risk tolerance does not change based on recent movements in the market (stocks, bonds, or real estate). The next best scenario would be that you decide to take more risk after the market has declined in value because prices are cheaper. The worst scenario is that you decide to take more risk after the markets have increased in value and prices are high. Unfortunately, that is what most people do.

### Do You Want to Make This Bet?

One example of changing risk tolerances can be seen in the way people gamble in a casino. Gamblers may come to Las Vegas with the mindset that they are ready, willing, and able to lose $1,000. They start out by betting $10 a hand on blackjack. What happens if they have a good run and turn their $1,000 into $4,000? They typically start making bigger bets. Now they are comfortable betting $50-$100 a hand. If they lose half of the $4,000, they have lost $2,000. However, they are not as upset as if they had lost their original $1,000. Why is that? It's because they feel like they were playing with the house's money. In other words, they never really believed that the $4,000 was their money. We see the same thing with investors who make quick money in investments. They typically increase their appetite for risk and end up giving most (if not all) of their gains back.

What about gamblers who early on have a bad run? They turn their $1,000 into $300. The majority of gamblers will change their behavior by moving from a $10 table to a $5 table or giving up on table games and heading over to the penny slots. In other words, gamblers do not have a process or system they stick with. They typically change their game or strategy based on short-term outcomes. Coincidentally, most investors do the same thing.

## Mutual Fund Flows Tell the Story

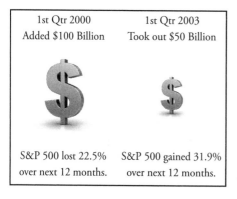

| 1st Qtr 2000 | 1st Qtr 2003 |
|---|---|
| Added $100 Billion | Took out $50 Billion |
| S&P 500 lost 22.5% over next 12 months. | S&P 500 gained 31.9% over next 12 months. |

It is easy to understand how someone might change his risk tolerance when gambling in a casino or betting on a coin toss. However, you would assume that people put more thought and planning into longer-term activities such as investing for retirement.

The question is: Do investors really change their long-term investment plan simply based on performance over the last month, last quarter, or year? Absolutely, they do. Look no further than a chart of mutual fund inflows and outflows. Early in the year 2000, stocks in the S&P 500 had just had one of their fastest and steepest increases in history. Valuations were very high and retail investors blew right through all the stop signs, dumping $100 billion of new money into retail mutual funds. The S&P 500 index lost 22.5% over the next 12 months. However, the downturn was just the beginning. Large cap domestic stocks lost money in 2000, 2001, and 2002. Stocks were once again reasonably valued after three years of double digit declines. So what did investors do now that stocks were on sale? That's right—they pulled their money out at the worst time. Investors withdrew $50 billion from mutual funds in the first quarter of 2003. The S&P 500 then gained 31.9% in the following 12 months and continued to climb over the next four years.

So our advice here is simple:

As long as you have a well-diversified, balanced portfolio that reflects your long-term goals, DO NOT PANIC and sell during a downturn. Even if you think you want less risk, make that change after your investments have recovered. It requires patience and discipline to wait to make these adjustments, but you can do it.

## PROTECTING YOUR EGO

> *"If you don't look facts in the face, they have a way of stabbing you in the back."*
> — Winston Churchill

Arguably the biggest motivator of mankind, after food and shelter, is ego. One thing that hurts your ego is making bad (and costly) decisions. Therefore, people often are more easily able to make decisions that make them feel good, and they are more likely to postpone those decisions that make them feel bad.

Consider a situation where you have invested in two stocks. One stock has increased in value by 20% and the other has decreased by 20%. Studies have shown that, on average, investors are 1.7 times more likely to sell the stock that has increased in value because it makes them feel good to lock in a profit. Realizing the gain will make you feel smart, and therefore, is good for your ego. However, what about the stock that has declined in value? You may show more reluctance to sell your losers because realizing the loss forces you to admit that you made a mistake. You can believe (or hope) that the stock price will rebound right up to the time you sell it. Continuing to hold the stock is a way to avoid regret. Similar situations occur in the real estate market when a person refuses to sell his house for less than he paid for it.

The tendency to sell winners and hold onto losers is known as the **Disposition Effect.**[7] Researchers have found the disposition effect to be pervasive with investors all over the world. In some countries, the average holding time for a losing stock trade was more than twice as long as the average holding time for a winning trade.

Does selling your profitable stock picks sooner and holding onto your unprofitable picks longer maximize your wealth? Unfortunately, research shows that the answer is, "No." In general, you would be

---

7   Source: Shapira, Zur and Itzhak Venezia. "Patterns of Behavior of Professionally Managed and Independent Investors." *Journal of Banking and Finance* 25 (2001): 1573-1587.

better off letting your winners run and selling your losing positions sooner. The lack of "sell" discipline is one of the biggest shortcomings we see in individual investors. There are two reasons why selling your winners early and holding onto your losers is not the wealth maximizing strategy:

Taxes: Selling your winners results in a capital gain, which is taxable (assuming it is not in an IRA or qualified retirement plan). In the spirit of full disclosure, we think it is a bad idea to continue to hold an investment that otherwise should be sold just to avoid taxes.

Future performance: Researcher Terrance Odean[8] conducted a study that analyzed 10,000 trading accounts from 1987-1993. He found that the "winners" (which were sold) beat the market by an average of 2.35% over the following year (after they were sold). The losers that were held underperformed the market by -1.06%.

Here is a good general rule for buy or sell decisions: Ask yourself, "If I had cash instead of the investment I already own, would I buy this same investment today?" If the answer is "No," then you should probably sell the investment instead of holding onto it, regardless of what you originally paid.

One other point you might find interesting is that investors feel stronger regret when the loss can be tied to their own decisions. Investors feel less regret about losses when they can blame a portfolio manager or financial advisor for the investment decision.

---

8   Source: Odean, Terrance. "Are Investors Reluctant to Realize their Losses?" *Journal of Finance* 53 (1998): 1775-1798.

## Memory and Your Positive Self-Image

Another aspect of protecting your positive self-image is selective memory and even mentally rewriting history. Picture someone who thinks of himself as smart but has a recollection of something he did that was not smart, or someone who thinks she is nice but did something that was not nice. The brain struggles with the two conflicting ideas. Psychologists call this uneasy feeling associated with conflicting ideas **cognitive dissonance**. People tend to dismiss or flat out reject any information that conflicts with their positive self-image. They partially do so on a deep subconscious level in order to resolve the uncomfortable feeling.

Consider people who are married and have done something dishonest such as having an affair or hiding money from a spouse. Such people may have thought of themselves as trustworthy but now they have done something untrustworthy. In most cases, they will rewrite the facts in their minds to justify their behavior. Marital therapists[9] tell us that frequently when wives cheat on their husbands, their behavior follows a predictable pattern. Initially, the woman seems to have all the things she wants—a home, a family, and a great husband, yet she feels she should be happier. She begins to question whether something is wrong with her because she feels unfulfilled. Eventually, she may have an affair because it is exciting, but it also leads to feelings of guilt or remorse. However, over time, the wife will become much more negative toward (and even angry at) her husband (the faithful spouse in this example). The cheating spouse's blame of the faithful spouse becomes much more pronounced *after* she has cheated because

9   Source: Langley, Michelle. *Women's Infidelity: Living In Limbo: What Women Really Mean When They Say "I'm Not Happy."* St. Louis, MO: McCarlan Publishing, 2005.

subconsciously she is trying to justify and reconcile her actions with her positive self-image. Whether it's a man or a woman who cheats, the need to view oneself with a positive self-image is the same.

Investors also change their beliefs to accommodate evidence that would be damaging to their self-images as smart investors. For example, let's say you buy a handful of mutual funds. Over time, the investments either do well or they don't. The performance information is published frequently and the wisdom of the original investment decisions becomes evident. If you are like most people, your brain will actually minimize negative information and focus on any positive information. That may sound silly, but many studies have verified the overly rosy recollection of individual investors.

In one such study, conducted by William Goetzmann and Nadav Peles[10], members of the American Association of Individual Investors were asked two questions related to their mutual fund holdings:

1. What was the return of your funds last year?

2. By how much did your mutual funds beat the market?

You would think investors who were part of an investment association would be actively involved in tracking their funds' performance and less prone to the behavioral biases of typical retail investors. However, the study found that these investors overestimated their actual return in a given year by 3.4 percentage points and overestimated their performance relative to the market index by 5.11 percentage points. This is just one example of how human memory adapts to ignore negative information.

---

10   Source: "Cognitive Dissonance and Mutual Fund Investors." *Journal of Financial Research* 20 (1997): 145-158.

We have often observed this same phenomenon when talking to prospective clients and analyzing their portfolios. A typical example plays out like this: a prospective client will tell us he is reasonably happy with his portfolio and figures he has earned 7-8% per year for the past decade. This rate of return may seem suspicious to us because the market has been flat for the last decade, and typically, an investor is not looking to hire someone if he has been highly successful on his own. Then we will look at his account statements, which show information such as original investment, contributions, withdrawals, and unrealized gains or losses. We then back test his holdings in order to quantify his portfolio's risk/volatility and past performance (which assumes he has been holding these same investments over the back test timeframe). The results tend to contradict his beliefs about his portfolio. Typically, the risk is much higher than he envisioned and the past returns are lower. The goal of this exercise is not to make the prospective client feel bad. The goal is to help him understand why we would make changes to his approach and the pitfalls of sticking with an investment plan that is not appropriate and/or not likely to be successful.

## THIS TIME IS DIFFERENT

> *"The only function of economic forecasting is to make astrology look respectable."*
> — John Kenneth Galbraith

Three things determine an investment's price: greed, fear, and valuations. In the long run, valuation wins out, but short-term, greed and fear can take the price of an investment far above or below its intrinsic value. Naturally, investors never think they are selling at a bad time because of fear or buying at a bad time based on greed. Instead, a number of mental biases hijack their logic (more on that in a moment).

Recently, at one of our firm's investment seminars, an attendee asked, "Did you foresee the recent real estate bubble's collapse?" The answer was "Yes," but unfortunately, we called the top too soon, as is usually the case. We were telling investors that real estate was overvalued 2-3 years before the top of the market. That statement made us look out of touch when real estate continued to skyrocket. However, we knew that the valuations were not sustainable. We just didn't know when the correction would hit. The same was true with the tech bubble of 2000-2002. We could see that large cap domestic stocks were trading at valuations that were not sustainable. The valuation of stocks in the S&P 500 index over the last 80 years has been approximately 15 times earnings. In other words, if a company had a profit of $1.00 per share, the stock price would be $15.00 per share. In early 2000, just before the market crash, the S&P 500 was trading at approximately 40 times earnings. It did not take a rocket scientist to figure out that large cap domestic stocks were overvalued.

So, if the long-term historical valuation of the S&P 500 was 15 times earnings, why did people continue to buy those stocks when they were valued at 25, 30, or 35 times earnings? Because investors always believe "It is different this time." Old methods of valuation do not apply because _____ (fill in the blank). With the tech crash, it was because the Internet was going to revolutionize the world. The rationale before the most recent real estate bubble was that home prices might level off but there would be no crash. People sat in our offices and told us, "I always make money on real estate" and "Real estate can't crash because people will always need a place to live" or "The cost of materials is skyrocketing so replacement cost is going up" or my personal favorite, "They aren't making any more land."

One woman actually told us in 2006 that she had just bought a rental property (in Las Vegas) that she was going to sell in four years to pay for her grandson's college. She figured she would have $100,000 in appreciation by then on her $250,000 purchase. It never occurred to her that four years later the house might be worth half what she paid for it, which is exactly what happened.

Sometimes being logical is lonely. It takes conviction and the threat of not being invited to as many cocktail parties to go against the herd. Warren Buffett is widely regarded as the world's most successful investor. However, many times people have written him off because he said things people didn't want to hear. Mr. Buffett was criticized for being out of touch during the tech boom of the late 1990s. People said he was a dinosaur for not getting on board with the idea that the old methods of valuing companies no longer applied in the Internet age. He took verbal abuse for a few years, but he was eventually vindicated when the tech bubble burst. In the October 16, 2008 issue of the *New York Times*, Buffett, the glutton for punishment that he is, wrote an op-ed piece titled "Buy American. I Am." He was going against the herd, which insisted that this time things were different. The financial system was on the verge of collapse so many thought the next Great Depression was beginning. Buffett was blasted again for being out of touch. Yet, Buffett stuck to his own advice: "Be *fearful when others are greedy*, and be *greedy when others are fearful*." He stated that although he couldn't predict the market's short-term direction, valuations were compelling, and it was a good time to buy stocks. Seven short months later, the market bottomed before doubling over the following 13 months.

Common characteristics exist for every investment bubble. It is easy to look back and recognize the two most recent investment bubbles we all experienced: the Internet bubble of the late 1990s and the real estate bubble of 2002-2007. However, if you lived in the 1850s, the bubble was related to the railroad. In the 1920s, it was the radio. In the 1940s and 1950s, it was because of the New Deal (economic reforms passed in the mid-1930s). In each case, large segments of the investing population decided the old methods of valuing companies did not apply anymore. This over-optimism and overconfidence led to great bull markets that ended very badly. It is easy to fool yourself that "It is different this time," but at the end of the day, valuations matter.

Your decisions may be wrong in the short run, but they will typically be proven right in time if your investment decisions are based on valuations. You will also avoid the fads and bubbles that destroy so many investors. If you ignore valuations and justify your decisions based on "other factors" you may be right in the short run, but frequently, you will end up going broke or losing a lot of your principal in the long run.

We also cannot stress enough the importance of good research. It is much easier to have conviction in your investments when you truly understand what you own and why you own it. Investing with conviction is more important than ever in today's volatile marketplace. More often than not, investors have virtually no information about a company's valuation, the management's efficiency, or even the outlook for the general sector. This lack of understanding is a primary reason why investors panic and sell at inopportune times. One negative statement about the company causes investors to second guess themselves. Make sure you can analyze a company's balance sheet properly before you invest one dollar in it. If you would like to read a good book on valuation, we recommend *Valuation: Measuring and Managing the Value of Companies*, co-authored by David Wessels, a professor at The Wharton Business School. Professor Wessels has an entertaining and unique way of teaching finance that translates well in this book.

# CHAPTER 2

# INVEST LIKE THE PROS

*"It's not whether you're right or wrong that's important,
but how much money you make when you're right and
how much you lose when you're wrong."*
— George Soros

Institutional investors (a.k.a. "The Pros")—such as pension funds and endowments—generally avoid many of the psychological biases and pitfalls that are so common among individual investors. One way they avoid human biases is by creating written Investment Policy Statements (IPS) that lay out some ground rules in advance for their investment decisions. The IPS includes their portfolio's objectives, their income distribution policy, a range of how much of the portfolio can be directed to various asset classes (asset allocation), and criteria for when (at what valuations and conditions) they will buy and sell. This written guideline is not developed during times of crisis. It is written when everyone is thinking clearly and enables institutional investors to focus on the long-term. As a result, these institutions frequently achieve higher "Risk-Adjusted" returns than individual investors.

Everyone would like higher returns. However, it may not be worth it if your attempt to earn higher returns requires you to take more risk. The goal for most investors is to get higher returns with the same (or preferably less) risk than they were taking previously. You cannot accurately compare the performance of two investments or two money managers simply by looking at past returns. You have to look at both returns and the risk taken to get those returns.

Let's say an investor walks into our office and says he earned 10% last year on his portfolio. Do we think that is a good return? The answer is…we don't know. It depends on how much risk he took to get that return. A 10% return is phenomenal if his portfolio had the same risk as a Treasury Bill (which is a 90-day loan to the U.S. Government). However, it's not a very good return if he had the real possibility of losing half of his money.

So, we have established that the Pros use a written Investment Policy in order to guide their decisions and minimize behavioral biases. What else do the Pros do differently? One thing is they commit to alternative asset classes (i.e. a more diverse set of investments).

**Alternative Asset Classes**

Most retail investors predominantly use traditional investments, which means that they own some combination of stocks, bonds, and cash. It is very difficult to attain significantly higher risk-adjusted returns by simply using these asset classes with a buy, hold, and rebalance approach. In today's economy, integrating alternative asset classes into your portfolio has never been more important.

What are alternative asset classes? Alternative investments include, but are not limited to: real estate, private equity, hedged equity, commodities, currencies, futures contracts, arbitrage, and absolute return.[1]

## Why Are Alternative Asset Classes So Important?

The two reasons why alternative asset classes are so important are that they:

1. <u>Provide growth during long-term cyclical bear markets</u> (when markets move sideways for many years): Many individual investors design their portfolios by looking in the rearview mirror. They feel they can count on stocks to deliver double digit returns because they are relying on statistics extrapolated from 80+ years of market data. However, what happens when you experience twelve years with zero returns in the stock market such as we have seen from 1999-2011? Even worse, what if the sideways market lasts for 16 years such as it did from 1966-1982, or 25 years from 1929-1954, or 18 years such as it did from 1906-1924. (see chart below)

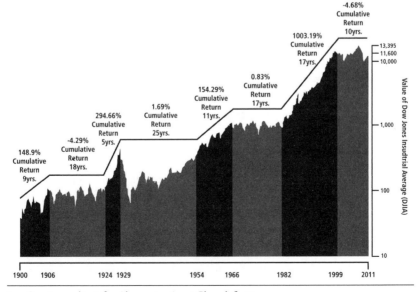

1  See Appendix A for Alternative Asset Class definitions

This scenario (a long-term sideways market) is even more devastating if you need to take distributions from the portfolio like most retirees, endowments, and pension funds. More and more retirees and mid to high net worth investors want consistent returns they can count on to provide systematic income in retirement. Endowments also need systematic income to support their institutions' operations.

2. Reduce Volatility: Thirty years ago, all you needed were stocks and bonds to have a diversified portfolio. However, it is important to understand that diversification does not mean that you simply hold many different investments. The key to diversification is to have a portfolio of investments that will not all decline at the same time. Therefore, you need some investments that go up when stocks and bonds are going down. Most major asset classes have become highly correlated over the last 30 years, meaning they now tend to move in the same direction. Institutions are relying on alternative asset classes to behave differently, in order to cushion downturns by going up (or even sideways) when the stock and bond markets have significant downturns.

**Why Focus on Consistent Results (Reducing Volatility)?**

One reason to reduce volatility is to minimize the extreme stresses that lead to poor decision-making. It is at market highs and lows that we see fear, greed, and the psychological biases we have discussed so far, hijack our otherwise good judgment.

A second reason is that "slow and steady" produces a better end result. Even the best money managers are going to have good years and bad years; however, by minimizing the severity of bad years, investors end up with higher compounding, which means a lot more money. Consider this example of the following two investors:

| Beginning account Value $1,000,000 | Investor A "Slow & Steady" | Investor B "Wild Ride" |
|---|---|---|
| Year 1 | 5% | 30% |
| Year 2 | 5% | -25% |
| Year 3 | 5% | 10% |
| Simple Avg Return | 5% | 5% |
| Compounded Avg Return | 5% | 2.36% |
| **Ending Value** | **1,157,620** | **1,072,500** |

They each have an average return of 5%, but Investor "A" ends up with much more money after just three years. This result happens because a portfolio with lower volatility compounds at a higher rate. The difference in the ending portfolio balance is even more pronounced if the account owners were taking distributions from the portfolio each year or if you look at a longer period of time.

For example, from 1950-2007 the S&P 500 produced a 9.19% average annual return. Over that same time period, an investment with the same simple average annual return, but half the volatility, would have produced 60% more wealth!

The institutional approach to investing is not designed to hit "home run" returns of 20-30% per year (although years like that can occur). Instead, it focuses on consistent compounding of more moderate gains to achieve greater results.

## Who Has Been Achieving Consistently High Risk Adjusted Returns?

The endowment funds of top universities such as Harvard and Yale have been pioneers in using non-traditional asset classes to produce higher and more consistent returns, and to achieve them with less volatility. Take a look at their results below:

### Results of the Endowment Approach to Investing[2]

| 1985-2008 | Annual compounded Rate of Return | Volatility (measured by Standard Deviation) |
|---|---|---|
| Yale & Harvard Endowments (Combined) | 15.95% | 9.75 α |
| S&P 500 | 11.98% | 15.6 α |

In 1980, Harvard's entire endowment fund was invested solely in domestic stocks and bonds. In 2010, those two asset classes (combined) only accounted for 15% of its endowment. So where had the other 85% gone? Some has gone into investments that are still considered traditional asset classes such as international and emerging market stocks and bonds. However, Harvard's largest allocations in 2011 are Absolute Return, Commodities, and Private Equity. In 2011,

2   Source: Faber, Mebane T. and Eric W. Richardson. *The Ivy Portfolio: How to Invest Like the Top Endowments and Avoid Bear Markets.* Hoboken, NJ: John Wiley & Sons, 2009.

NOTE: Standard Deviation(α) measures the variation in returns from the average. A low standard deviation shows consistency; higher standard deviation indicates wild swings.

the average endowment fund has 57% of its portfolio allocated to alternative investments, yet the average retail investor has less than 10% in alternatives.

## Harvard Endowment Results vs. Benchmarks[3]

|  | 10 year returns (through 2009) | 20 year returns (through 2009) |
|---|---|---|
| **Harvard Endowment** | 8.9% | 11.7% |
| **S&P 500** | -.99% | 8.23% |
| **Typical 60% stock / 40% bond portfolio** | 1.4% | 7.8% |

A great book for investors interested in learning more about the endowment approach to investing is *Pioneering Portfolio Management* by David Swensen. Mr. Swensen is the Chief Investment Officer for the Yale endowment and has an extraordinary track record.

---

3   Sources: *Harvard Gazette*, January 2010, www.hmc.harvard.edu; S&P annual return from Yahoo Finance.

# CHAPTER 3

# REDUCE INVESTMENT RISK WITHOUT REDUCING RETURNS

---

*"Everyone has a plan until they get hit."*
– Mike Tyson

## Risk Management Systems

In addition to using alternative asset classes, most institutional investors have systems that they follow for managing risk and deciding when and at what price to buy and sell various investments.

The multiple booms and busts of the last 15 years have laid bare the shortcomings of relying too much on asset allocation and a strict buy and hold strategy. In fact, the top investors are the ones who know how to incorporate current valuations and world events into a cohesive risk management strategy. In other words, they have a plan to hedge or reduce their exposure to certain asset classes when the risks outweigh the potential rewards.

Risk Management cannot (or at least should not) be done based on "gut feel" or emotion. Your system for reducing exposure must be quantifiable and determined in advance. It is important to understand that in this day and age, you can protect yourself from market downturns. However, that protection comes at a price, which can be a drag on your returns. Therefore, you have to hedge (or protect yourself from) the right risks at the right price. Think of that protection as insurance. Most institutional investors budget a certain amount each year for options, derivatives, or other tools that essentially act as "portfolio insurance." Institutional investors realize that you do not need to participate in 100% of the upside as long as you protect yourself from a good portion of the downside.

We have noticed that investors tend to become complacent with risk when markets are stable and trending upward, such as we witnessed from 2003-2007. It's in years like 2008, when we saw U.S. stocks decline 40%, that investors are reminded of the critical need to understand and minimize their investment risk. As Warren Buffett once said, "YOU only *find out* who is *swimming* naked when the *tide goes out*."

Unfortunately, many individual and professional investors alike fail to implement a comprehensive risk management strategy. Most risk management strategies are an afterthought and a good example of "too little, too late." Failing to adopt a risk management plan from day one can cause investors to become paralyzed in rapidly falling markets.

Experienced risk analysts, money managers, and stock and bond traders will tell you that individual investments can fail even when you have done all of the research and have all of the data on your side. The key to successful investing is to make sure the size of your failures does not outweigh the size of your successes. So the question is: How do you limit the size of your investment mistakes in order to achieve the highest return for the lowest risk?

## Diversification Is Not Enough

Asset allocation (sometimes referred to as diversification) is not enough to protect you in a volatile economy. The problem is that during a severe downturn or financial panic, all major asset classes can decline at the same time. For instance, Long Term Capital Management was a hedge fund managed by two Nobel Laureates. They had some of the most sophisticated models in the world and yet ultimately failed miserably. One of the core flaws was that they relied too much on diversification. They failed to recognize the size of the ripple effects on many of their investments after Russia devalued its currency.

Many investment professionals also saw the subprime mortgage problem years in advance. What many failed to understand was the ensuing liquidity crisis that would cause the value of just about every investible asset class to collapse simultaneously in the second half of 2008. Once again, diversification failed. We are not trying to show by these examples that diversification is a bad thing; only that it is not enough.

There is no such thing as a risk-free portfolio. Risk exists on many levels, whether you invest too conservatively or too aggressively. But there are steps investors can take to help protect their portfolios.

## SEVEN STEPS TO A LOWER-RISK PORTFOLIO

### Step 1: Create an "Efficient Portfolio"

We like to call this strategy the only free lunch in investing. Harry Markowitz first introduced Modern Portfolio Theory (MPT) in an article in 1952. He was later awarded the Nobel Prize in economics in 1990. MPT explains how you can combine different types of investments (often called asset classes) in order to reduce risk without reducing returns. This debunked the notion that you had to accept more risk if you wanted higher returns. The idea is to combine investments that all have positive long-term trends but don't all go up or down at the same time.

Let's look at an example: assume Bond Portfolio A and Stock Portfolio B have average returns of 6% and 12.5% respectively, and a standard deviation (a measure of volatility) of 7.5% and 15% respectively. There are times when stocks go up while bonds' values are declining and vice versa. Therefore, blending a portfolio of stocks and bonds in various proportions may reduce volatility as demonstrated in the chart below[1]:

| Percent A (% in Bonds) | Percent B (% in Stocks) | Portfolio Average Return | Volatility (Std Deviation) |
|---|---|---|---|
| 100% | 0% | 6.00% | 7.50% |
| 90% | 10% | 6.65% | 7.34% |
| 80% | 20% | 7.30% | 7.47% |
| 70% | 30% | 7.95% | 7.87% |
| 60% | 40% | 8.60% | 8.51% |
| 50% | 50% | 9.25% | 9.34% |
| 0% | 100% | 12.5% | 15% |

This example illustrates that it would be preferable to have the portfolio with 80% bonds and 20% stocks vs. a portfolio with 100% in bonds. That's because the portfolio with 20% in stocks has *both a higher return and lower risk*. However, it is not always preferable

---

1    Example adapted from *BISYS Review for the CFP Certification examination.* 9th ed. 2005

for a given investor to go to 30% stocks and 70% bonds because while it would further increase the return, it would increase the risk, which may be unacceptable to the investor. Far too often we see retail investors who don't truly have a "portfolio." Their investments were not selected based on how they worked together, but rather they are a collection of investments that were sold to them without regard to how well the investments complemented one another.

Several software resources online can help you to create an "efficient" portfolio. The planned percentage you decide to put in each asset class is referred to as your "strategic asset allocation." This allocation is determined by historical data that shows how the prices of each asset class move in various market conditions. You should recognize, however, that an efficient portfolio is just the first step.

### Step 2: Overweighting or Underweighting Asset Classes Based on Current Market Conditions and Valuations.

As mentioned above, the strategic allocation is how assets move based on *past* data. It does not necessarily mean they will move that way in the future. Current events and valuations also need to be taken into consideration.

For example, suppose our plan is to have 15% of your portfolio in U.S. large company stocks. However, U.S. large company stocks are currently overvalued relative to other asset classes, like they were in the late 1990s. We would reduce the percentage we invest there and move some of that money to an asset class that is undervalued. Once the valuations of U.S. large company stocks drop, we could then move back to the 15% allocation. On the flip side, if we see deep value in

U.S. stocks, we may decide to invest a higher percentage of assets in this area. Active money managers are constantly making these types of overweighting and underweighting decisions and reassessing risk and reward for each area of their clients' portfolios.

## Step 3: Pairing Passive and Active Strategies

Steps one and two have helped determine what percentage of your money should be allocated to the different investment areas at any given time. The next step is to choose the specific investments for each area. What specific individual investments should be used to fulfill the commodities allocation, the emerging market debt, the managed futures, the real estate, the U.S. small cap stocks, and so forth?

Some money managers believe in **passive management**, which means they only use investments that are designed to mirror the performance of an entire category of the market such as large company U.S. stocks (typically using Index Funds or Exchange Traded Funds). The alternative is **active management** where you pick individual stocks, bonds, or other investments you feel will provide more upside potential or less risk than investing broadly in the entire category. Both active and passive management have pros and cons. Our firm uses both passive and actively managed investments. This approach enables us to have the broad diversification of investing in a category (also known as the index), but it also enables us potentially to outperform or minimize risk by investing in individual companies that we expect to hold up well in the face of certain challenges (e.g. high inflation, credit crunch, etc.). We firmly believe that active risk management will be necessary for anyone looking to achieve superior risk-adjusted returns in the foreseeable future.

## Step 4: Limiting Position Size

You can only lose what you invest. Enron, WorldCom, and other such disasters remind us that position size is critical. If Enron were only 1% of your portfolio, you could have made that loss back in a day or two with normal market fluctuations. If Enron were 25% of your portfolio, it would probably take several years to recover that loss. We strongly recommend that you limit position sizes to no more than 3-5% in any individual company.

## Step 5: Daily Monitoring

You or your advisor should be able to react at a moment's notice to real time market information. Should an accounting scandal arise, you may have only moments to react to specific news. If you are not able to devote this type of time, then here are two simple recommendations:

- Do not use individual stocks; instead mutual funds or exchange traded funds (ETF's).

- If you choose to ignore recommendation #1, then use "stop loss" orders, which trigger your investment to sell automatically if it falls below a certain price.

Active investment professionals almost never use stop loss orders, but they can be appropriate for someone who is not willing or able to follow his or her investments all day, every day (in other words, if you have a life, unlike the authors of this book).

Keep in mind that stop loss orders have limitations and can be disastrous if stocks suddenly experience a sharp decline. Your sale price can end up being significantly less than your stop order because when your stock hits the trigger price, your stock will sell for whatever you can get at that moment. For example, let's say you own shares of IBM at $175 per share and you place a stop order at $170. If the stock reports bad news after hours, it could open up at $150 so that is where you would be selling. Many times, the market overreacts and the stock quickly recovers. However, if you got stopped out, then you are out of the stock.

An order called a **stop limit** allows you to place a limit price below the stop. Let's assume a stop at $170 with a limit of $160. The risk here, using our example of opening at $150, is that the order would never execute and the stock could continue to plummet without selling. For that reason, in our opinion, ETF's and mutual funds are a much better choice for "do-it-yourself" investors. Individual stocks are more appropriate for people who can afford the time to watch the market each day.

### Step 6: Thorough Research

Many investors too often become married to one method of analyzing investments. However, we believe that the more information you have, the better. Our approach uses three different types of analysis: quantitative (numbers and ratios), fundamental (products, markets, and management), and technical (price movement and trading volume). When using all three types of analysis, you are better able to identify investments where valuations are compelling, management and business models are superior, and technically, volumes and money flow confirm your conclusions.

## Step 7: Hedging Market Risk

Keep in mind that no position is better than to own an all-stock portfolio in a bull market, except for an all-stock portfolio you have borrowed against to buy even more stock (a leveraged all stock portfolio). The problem is that a bull market is never recognized until it's in the rearview mirror. You never know, until after the fact, when one starts and when one ends. Buying portfolio protectors (such as put options) or negatively correlated funds (which go up when the stock market goes down) to insure your portfolio typically aren't great investments. It's like purchasing fire insurance for your home. It's a lousy investment. Do you have fire insurance on your home? We do. As an investment it has a negative net present value, which is tough to accept as an investment analyst. It is one dumb investment, UNLESS you own a house. Then it makes a lot of sense! It would be great if you could time when your house was going to burn down, and then buy the insurance the day before. Unfortunately, without stiff legal consequences, that isn't possible. It's the same thing with buying portfolio protection. It is a drag in good years, but you're glad you had it in years like 2008.

Every once in awhile, our financial markets experience a severe correction, such as we saw in 2008. These corrections can drive down asset prices far lower than what we determine to be their "fair value." The "buy and hold" strategy can be devastating in times like these. You can reduce volatility in your portfolio and protect yourself from steep corrections by having some portfolio insurance. The most common way to hedge (i.e. insure) investments in the stock market is through the use of **put options** that give you the right to sell your investment at a pre-determined price any time prior to the options expiration date.

One final point about using portfolio insurance: it enables you to invest more aggressively than would be appropriate without the insurance. Therefore, you can capture more of the upside in bull markets, which frequently outweighs the cost of the insurance. In other words, having an aggressive portfolio with some hedges frequently provides better risk-adjusted returns than the typical conservative portfolio without any hedges. Unfortunately, most retail investors and their financial advisors never use hedges because they require a fair amount of time and expertise to manage. Nevertheless, high net worth investors, hedge funds, pension funds, and other institutional investors use them regularly.

Another way to manage risk is to use technical analysis to try to identify steep declines early (market timing) and reduce your exposure. These technical indicators, such as moving averages, Fibonacci levels, pattern recognition and the like, work great...until they don't. You could easily go broke if your whole strategy were based on these patterns that did not work out as expected. The people who use such tools often tout the small losses they take using stop orders and moving averages. What they fail to mention is that forty "small" 2% losses is 80% of your portfolio. If you want to spend a day with us, we can show you chart after chart of foolproof patterns that didn't work. Robert had the privilege early in his career as a proprietary trader of seeing firsthand the profit and loss statements of traders who wrote the books on technical analysis. He can tell you there is a reason why these people are selling books and not living on their "Holy Grail" trading patterns. This example shows why it is foolish and overly simplistic for financial "professionals" to manage clients' retirement money based entirely on technical indicators (i.e. charts). That is not to say that technical analysis doesn't have a role to play. It should be one of the many tools you use in your decision process, just not the only one.

## Final Thoughts on Risk Management

The role of professional money managers has changed. The new paradigm is that the "upside," for the most part, will take care of itself. The measure of good investment professionals is how well they manage downside risk. You cannot control how far or fast markets will rise; nor do you need to. However, you can control how far you are willing (and able) to let your portfolio fall. For example, large institutional investors, such as pension funds, know in advance how far they can let their portfolios decline before it compromises their ability to meet their obligations. They frequently spend as much time (or more) in determining how to protect against downturns as they do in figuring out where to invest their money. As an individual investor, you may face many of the same challenges as a pension fund or endowment. For example, you may need to provide inflation-adjusted income for one or more people's lives. Similar to a pension fund, you can only tolerate a certain amount of downside exposure and still be able to recover in order to meet your long-term obligations. Therefore, you need to have a plan to manage risk or at least know how much risk you can afford to take. We recommend that you do not attempt to track indexes or find hot stocks that can make or break you. You will be much further ahead if you can simply capture a good percentage of the upside while significantly limiting your downside.

# CHAPTER 4

# RETIREMENT IN AMERICA TODAY

*"You know you are getting old when caution is
the only thing you wish to exercise."*
— Algie Petrere

Retirement is supposed to be the point at which one stops living at work and starts working at life. Retirement should be a time to pursue hobbies, travel, and activities you never had time for when you were working. Alternatively, you can stick around the house and drive your spouse nuts (not that we know anyone who does that). Naturally, an active and fulfilling retirement is much more attainable if you are financially prepared for retirement. Unfortunately, the average retiree in America spends a great deal of time worrying about money. We have included the statistics below to give you an idea of just how unprepared the average American is for retirement. We also know that the people most likely to read this book are more affluent than the general population, and therefore, not representative of these statistics. Hopefully, knowing how much better you are doing than the median household in America makes you feel fortunate. If you are younger, perhaps these statistics will encourage you to save more so you are prepared when your time comes.

In a survey[1] of 3,257 U.S. adults in May of 2010, 92% felt that we have a retirement crisis in this country. Fewer employers are offering pension plans, employees are not saving nearly enough for retirement, Social Security only replaces a fraction of the income most retirees will need and people are living longer. That is a bad combination of circumstances. Consider these statistics:

- According to a 2011 JP Morgan Research study, Americans are dangerously underestimating how much money they will need in retirement. Nearly half of respondents thought they would need less than 75% of their pre-retirement salary, yet extensive research shows that retirees spend more than that. To make matters worse, only 40% of those pre-retirees believe they will be able to reach their (unrealistically low) financial goals.[2]

In our practice, we very seldom see our retirees spending less than they did pre-retirement. Many actually spend more because they are traveling more, golfing more, and spending more on health care. They are also spending time with the grandkids, which can be expensive, especially if they're anything like my three year-old who has already talked me into buying her an iPad. Thankfully, we own Apple stock!

- The average household's pre-retirement income that will be replaced by Social Security is projected to fall from 39% in 2002 to 28% by 2030, due to the increase in the Social

---

1   Source: Larson Research and Strategy Consulting, Inc and DSS Research nationwide online survey, Reclaiming the Future.
2   Source: JP Morgan Retirement Plan Service, white paper "Searching for Certainty" (June 2011).

Security Full Retirement Age (FRA) and higher Medicare deductions.[3]

- Only 1 in 5 workers today is covered by a traditional pension. The share of private-sector workers covered by a defined benefit pension plan has declined from 39% in 1980 to less than 20% today.[4]

- In 2007, near the peak of the stock market, half of households approaching retirement (ages 55-64) had less than $98,000 in a retirement savings account (that's if they had an account at all; the median for all households was much lower). The increased personal responsibility for retirement savings is making retirees more vulnerable to market turbulence. In 2007, $98,000 would have only been enough to purchase an annuity that would pay $5,400 a year for the remainder of both spouses' lives. That would only replace 10% of these households' median income.[5]

Hopefully, you are much better prepared for retirement than the average American. Nevertheless, you are *not* home free simply because you were successful at accumulating assets in the first half (or two-thirds) of your life.

3   Source: Munnell, Alicia H., Anthony Webb and Francesca Golub-Sass, "The National Retirement Risk Index: After the Crash." Figure 4. *Center for Retirement Research*. Number 9-22 (October 2009): 2.
4   Source: Cushing-Daniels, Brendan and Richard W. Johnson. "Employer-Sponsored Pensions: A Primer." *The Retirement Policy Project*. Urban Institute, Income and Benefits Policy Center (January 2008) p. 3.
5   Sources: Bucks, Brian K., Arthur B. Kennickell, Traci L. Mack, and Kevin B. Moore. "Changes in U.S. Family Finances from 2004 to 2007: Evidence from the Survey of Consumer Finances." *Federal Reserve Board*. (February 2009) p. A5, A19, and Morrissey, Monique. "Toward a universal, secure, and adequate retirement system." *Retirement USA Conference Report*. Economic Policy Institute (October 21, 2009) p. 18.

Ten years ago, I (Jeremy) was having dinner at a restaurant in La Jolla, California with a friend who had a relatively successful business. He has always been particularly insightful and someone I long considered a mentor. As we were talking about his financial goals, he said, "You know, you can't eat in a much nicer restaurant than this. You can't drive a much nicer car than the one I drive now. You can't live in a much nicer place than this. So, yeah I want to make more money, but I am not willing to sacrifice my health, my sanity, or my time with my family."

I was really surprised to hear him say that because this friend is an entrepreneur, someone I thought of as a risk-taker, and he was still relatively young. That conversation changed my perspective and helped me understand the important shift in mindset from wealth accumulation to lifestyle preservation. We know a lot of people reading this book have lifestyles they love (i.e. their home, family and friends, health, the ability to travel, and the freedom to buy most of the things they want). We also see too many people who had enough money to retire and be comfortable for the rest of their lives, but they lost or wasted much of it due to bad investments and a lack of planning. The insights in this book can help you avoid such a fate.

Three of the main challenges associated with planning for retirement are the uncertainty surrounding:

- Your life expectancy

- Inflation

- Future healthcare costs

We provide some food for thought on each of these important topics on the next few pages.

## LIFE EXPECTANCY

*"You can live to be 100 if you give up all the things that make you want to live that long."*

— Woody Allen

The average life expectancy has been under 30 for almost the entire time mankind has walked this earth. It only started to rise in a significant and sustained way in the last few hundred years. The average life expectancy in the United States increased to 38 years by 1800. It was 47 years by 1900, 76.5 years by 2000, and 78.3 by 2010[6]. Since the end of World War II, life expectancy has been increasing by an average of two months every year. It is no wonder that our pension systems and Social Security are going broke! In fact, when Social Security was originally passed into law in 1935, the Full Retirement Age was 65 years old and the average life expectancy was only 61.7!

Today, the average retiree spends over 20 years in retirement. However, you know what they say about averages, "If you have one foot in boiling water and the other in ice water, on average you should be comfortable." In other words, it is often dangerous to rely on averages. Despite our warnings about relying on averages, we have included the chart[7] below to show how likely it is for an "average" 65 year-old to live well into his or her 80s or 90s.

6   Source: U.S. Census Bureau
7   Source: Jordan, Joseph W., Dan Weinberger, and Joel L. Franks. White Paper: "Engaging Clients in a New Way: Putting the Findings of Behavioral Finance Strategies to Work." New York: Metlife, 2011.

| Retirement Age | | 50% Chance of Living Beyond | 25% Chance of Living Beyond |
|---|---|---|---|
| 65 | Male | 86 years | 92 years |
| 65 | Female | 88 years | 94 years |
| 65 | Couple (at least one spouse has a chance of living beyond) | 92 years | 97 years |

You can see by the chart above that a 65 year-old couple has a 50% probability that one or the other spouse will live to age 92 or beyond. The same couple has a 25% chance that one will live to age 97. Keep in mind that these probabilities are based on the entire population, including those who are obese, chain smokers, and those who already have serious medical conditions. Living into your 90s may sound like a long life. However, you may be surprised to find out that an estimated 104,754 centenarians (people 100 years or older) were alive in the U.S. as of November 2009.[8]

Most people want to live a long, healthy life. What they frequently don't understand is that their biggest financial risk is living too long. Imagine the financial situation of each of these centenarians if they had relied on a retirement plan based on them living to the average life expectancy or even an extra five or ten years. A little closer to home...some of the people reading this book will live to be 100 or more. Will one of them be you?

---

8   Source: Bureau of the Census. "Facts for Features." March 2, 2010.

Other considerations in estimating longevity[9]:

- People who are Caucasian tend to live longer than minorities (except Asians).

- People who are educated tend to live longer than those who are not.

- People with higher incomes tend to live longer than those with lower incomes.

So, if you are a thin, educated, non-smoker with financial resources, you have a very good chance of outliving the averages.

You can estimate your life expectancy based on your personal situation (health, habits, diet, weight, family history, etc.) at **www.livingto100.com**. Their life expectancy calculator is based on a free survey that will take you about 10 minutes to complete.

You must be thinking that with the retirement savings crisis and the population living longer, that most people would continue to work for a few more years. Wrong. People have actually been retiring earlier. Over the last 60 years, the average age at which Americans retire has trended downward by more than five years from 66.9 to 61.6. Furthermore, almost 40% are forced to retire earlier than planned due to company downsizing, layoffs, or medical disabilities.[10]

---

9   Source: *Journal of Financial Planning.* Dec 2008.
10  Source: Bureau of Labor Statistics.

In the Income Planning section of this book, we will address the best way to make your money last, but for now, let's get a better understanding of two other retirement challenges: inflation and healthcare costs.

## INFLATION

*"I don't mind going back to daylight savings time. With inflation, the hour will be the only thing I've saved all year."*
— Victor Borge

Inflation is a silent killer. It is the most underestimated threat to a retiree's lifestyle. Imagine if all prices remained stable for five years at a time and then jumped up by 15-20% all at once. This price increase would occur on a single day at the end of every five year period. People would be worrying about it, talking about it, and planning for it. However, it doesn't work like that. It creeps up slowly and unevenly. Some products have not experienced any inflation over the past five years (e.g. computers, cameras, cell phones). Other products have had dramatic price increases (e.g. healthcare, education). You don't even realize that inflation is happening in many cases. Gas prices are an exception because the price is plastered on big signs on every street corner. However, if you ask how much has the price increased over the past five years for butter, paper, cereal, electricity, most people have no idea.

As of the writing of this book, general consumer inflation as measured by the Consumer Price Index (CPI) has been cruising along in the 2-3% range. These calculations are according to the U.S. government and would seem to indicate that inflation is nothing to worry about.

However, anyone who does grocery shopping has noticed lately that prices are rising much more than 2-3%. In fact, in the past year, the price of ground beef is up 11.1%, coffee is up 16.6% and butter is up over 27%. Luckily, bread prices are only up 3%, so you may want to reconsider your feelings about dry toast.

One of the reasons the CPI seems to understate inflation is that 42% of the CPI is housing costs. If you look at "core inflation," which backs out food and energy, then housing is over 50% of the index. That difference may explain why the government statistics on inflation don't seem to jive with your spending experiences. Most people don't spend 42-50% of their income on housing. Many retirees own their homes and no longer have a mortgage, so housing costs have almost no relevance to their household budget and spending.

Anyway, here is the point we want to make about inflation: if you would like to maintain your standard of living during retirement, you need a plan that increases your income each year to keep pace with inflation. Some pensions have Cost of Living Adjustments (COLA's), as does Social Security. However, many pensions do not adjust for inflation; nor do most annuities, bonds, or CDs.

One more example to drive this point home: Let's assume that you retired in January of 1986 with a plan to live on $80,000 per year. Let's also assume that $30,000 of that was covered by Social Security and/or pensions (with COLA's) and $50,000 was to be funded by withdrawals from your savings. By the end of 2010, you would need to have increased the withdrawals from your savings to $100,465 in order to cover the 100.93% inflation that had occurred over your 25 year retirement.[11]

| How Prices Change Over a 25 Year Retirement | | |
|---|---|---|
| Cost of Living Numbers | 2010 | 1986 |
| Item | Price/Level | Price/Level |
| New Car | $29,217 | $9,255 |
| New House | $268,700 | $89,430 |
| Gallon of Milk | $2.79 | $1.59 |
| Gallon of Gas | $2.73 | $0.89 |
| Loaf of Bread | $2.49 | $0.55 |
| Dow Jones (DJIA) | 11,577 | 1,895 |

[12]

## HEALTHCARE COSTS

Let us begin our healthcare discussion by saying that like most people, we dislike talking about long-term care (LTC). However, no book on retirement and investing would be complete without it. The reality is that healthcare is one of the biggest potential future expenses that can really torpedo the best laid retirement plans. First, a quick background: Medicare is going to cover the majority of your medical expenses. Part A covers hospitalization. Part B covers traditional doctor visits/tests and part D covers most of your prescription drug costs. Naturally, there are deductibles and co-pays, which are inconvenient but not likely to wipe you out.

The big problem is that Medicare does not cover long-term care, which is the care necessary when you are not able to take care of

---

11 Source: www.inflationdata.com, inflation figures based on CPI-U, which includes food and energy.
12 Sources: www.thepeoplehistory.com/pricebasket.html, http://bigcharts.marketwatch.com

yourself (bathing, eating, going to the bathroom, getting out of bed, etc.). This type of care is most frequently provided at home by family members, then by home health aides, and ultimately (as a last resort), at nursing homes. We said that Medicare does not cover LTC, but that is a bit of an over-simplification. Medicare will cover the first 20 days if you were transferred from a hospital (where you stayed for at least three days) directly to an LTC facility. After the first 20 days, you begin paying a co-pay (which at the present time is $130 per day) for the next 80 days with Medicare picking up anything above the co-pay. You are on your own after 100 days. It should also be noted that Medicare only covers "skilled nursing care"; anything less (i.e. non-medical care) is not covered.

## The Quick Statistics on Long-Term Care:

- Approximately 1 in 2 adults who are age 65 today will need LTC at some point during the remainder of their lives. Remember that LTC includes in-home care as well as nursing home.

- The average time someone receives care in his or her home is 11 months. However, in many cases a person's condition worsens so he or she has to be admitted to a nursing home where the average stay is 2.4 years.

- The biggest financial threat is cognitive impairment (Alzheimer's, Parkinson's, Dementia). One third to one half (depending on which study you believe) of people over the age of 85 develop cognitive impairment. The average time people with cognitive impairment need care is 9 years!

- The average cost of non-medical home healthcare is $21 per hour. Some people need help a few hours a day; others need 24-hour care.

- The average cost of a nursing home nationwide is $247 per day ($7,400 per month) for a private room, but keep in mind that all of these costs vary substantially depending on your geographic location.

- Since 2004, the average cost of LTC has been increasing 4.4-6.6% per year depending on the category of care. General inflation (CPI) has only been 2.5% per year during that timeframe.

Once you spend (almost) all of your money, you can qualify for a welfare program called Medicaid. Single people trying to qualify for Medicaid can only keep $2,000 in non-exempt assets. If you are married, the applicant's spouse is able to keep half of the couple's non-exempt assets up to a maximum of $109,560 (this amount does change from time to time and may be different at the time you are reading this book). The major assets that are exempt include one car, your house (up to $500,000 in value), burial plots for you and your spouse, and your wedding ring. Income requirements and lots of fine print can also inhibit your ability to qualify for Medicaid. Entire books and websites are dedicated to this topic, so obviously, we are just including a quick overview here. The bottom line is that until you have depleted your assets to the levels specified, you will have to "spend down" your own money on this care. That includes cashing in your IRAs, cash value life insurance, investment portfolio, annuities, CDs, selling your vacation home, etc. You get the idea.

It isn't pretty and is basically the very last thing you ever wanted to spend your money on. In essence, Medicaid is a welfare program. So at this point, you probably want to throw yourself in front of a fast moving bus in order to cheer yourself up. We recommend that you do not do that, especially since there is some good news. The good news is that the range of potential financial solutions for LTC has never been better. Many people do not want to buy LTC insurance because it is expensive and most people are in denial—they believe they will never need it.

If you have less than $200,000 in total (non-exempt) assets, it may make sense to take your chances. If you need LTC, then you would liquidate and spend your assets on your medical care until you qualify for Medicaid. The only caveat is that you will not leave much (if anything) behind for your beneficiaries. Nevertheless, we could see how that decision would make sense for some people with less than $200,000 in non-exempt assets and limited income available to pay for LTC insurance. If you have more than $1.5 million in non-exempt assets, you may want to self-insure. In other words, you could take your chances because you figure that even at $60-$120,000 per year, a typical LTC scenario is not going to wipe you out.

We are *not* blindly recommending that you don't insure if you have less than $200,000 or that you self-insure if you have more than $1.5 million. It is just that those decisions make sense for many of the people we have met. The people who need a long-term care solution the most are those in the middle with $200,000-$1.5 million in assets. This is especially true for couples because if one spouse gets sick, it could leave the surviving spouse without any significant assets for the rest of his or her life.

## Hybrid Insurance Solutions

Traditional LTC insurance is alive and well and is arguably the best solution to protect against an extended care event, especially if you are young (under 65) and healthy. However, the fastest growing trend in LTC is hybrid solutions or asset-based LTC insurance. These hybrid solutions are essentially life insurance or annuities that provide a pool of money if an extended care event should take place. The reason for their popularity is that you can access cash values and/or death benefits if the policy is not used to pay for LTC (home healthcare or nursing home). Most of these products also have simplified underwriting that does not require an examination or medical records.

Let's look at an example: one popular solution is a single premium life insurance product. A 65 year-old female (standard rate class) can deposit $100,000 into the policy and have an immediate death benefit of $150,000. If she needs LTC, the policy will provide up to $450,000 to pay for LTC expenses ($6,250 per month for up to six years). You are essentially spending the life insurance death benefit while you are still alive to pay for LTC. If you spend all of the death benefit, then the insurance company continues to pay your expenses (up to three times your original death benefit). The policy also pays a minimum residual death benefit of 10%. That means that even if the policy holder in our example used up the $150,000 or more for LTC expenses, her beneficiary would still receive at least $15,000. Another nice feature of this product is the return of premium guarantee, which means the policyholder can change his or her mind at any time after the policy is issued and walk away with no less than the original deposit ($100,000 in this example).

The previous example was a life insurance product, but there are also annuities with LTC riders that work in a similar manner. One annuity product is even designed to provide lifetime income for one or both spouses. However, if either spouse cannot perform two of the six activities of daily living (ADL's), then the insurance company will double the income payout of the annuity for up to five years. This income can also be used for home healthcare (you do not need to be confined to a nursing home). Let's suppose the following happens: the sick spouse passes away and the annuity's cash value has been depleted. The insurance company will then continue the regular lifetime income payments to the surviving spouse for the rest of his or her life.

In summary, healthcare costs are one of the big unknowns in retirement. The bad news is that one day you may need help taking care of yourself (or your spouse). The good news is that, with a little planning, you can ensure that your life savings will not depleted.

# CHAPTER 5

# INCOME PLANNING

*"I have enough money to last me the rest of my life,*
*unless I buy something."*
– Jackie Mason

## WHAT'S YOUR NUMBER?

In our business, we meet people with millions of dollars who are afraid to spend any of it and also people who are blowing through their savings at rates that are clearly unsustainable. Spending is certainly an area where we see various degrees of irrationality. We don't make any judgments regarding what people should spend their money on. You earned it so you should spend it how you wish. Just  make sure you don't spend your last dollar before you take your last breath. One retiree told us his retirement plan was to bounce his last check to the nursing home. That sounds great, but just in case you don't know exactly how long you're going to live, you might want to have an income plan that errs on the side of having some money left over.

Most people do not have a good grasp on how much they need to save for retirement or how much they can afford to withdraw from their savings once they are retired. Generally, individuals will need the assistance of a financial planner to help them accurately determine how much money they need to retire comfortably. Experienced financial planners use a variety of software programs to analyze and project possible financial outcomes and probabilities of success.

The number one goal of most retirees is to make sure they have enough money when they retire so they will never run out. Some retirees have secondary goals such as leaving a financial legacy for their heirs or donating money to certain charities. Developing a financial plan forces you to think through many important aspects of your future. Most people feel much more at ease about their future once they have a financial plan that can serve as a roadmap and reduce uncertainty.

In order to prepare meaningful and useful projections, you should have the following information with you when you meet with a financial planner:

1. Your List of Assets and Liabilities: Be sure to include any business interests, real estate holdings, and the balance as well as the type of all accounts (e.g. 401k, brokerage account, trust account, individual savings account, etc). You should include your home as an asset and your mortgage as a liability.

2. Estimate of Needed Income: This estimate is the most important part of the retirement planning process. Many pre-retirees we meet have not spent much time developing an accurate estimate for how much they will spend each year in

retirement. We have seen clients who estimate they will spend $8,000 per month when the actual figure turns out to be over $10,000. That may not seem like a big deal, but when you plan to generate inflation adjusted-income over a 20-40 year period, significantly underestimating your income needs can destroy your chances of success. As a result, we frequently spend time with clients, making a spreadsheet of all of their expected expenses and helping them think through some of the financial choices they will make during retirement. One of our clients had his retirement spending planned down to which magazine subscriptions he was going to keep. Clearly, this client is the exception and that level of detail may not be necessary (although we loved it!).

In the past, many financial planners assumed that you would spend 70-90% of your pre-retirement income once you were retired. However, today's retirees are enjoying longer, and more active retirements, and spending more money as a result. Therefore, we find that the appropriate range is really 70-110% of your pre-retirement income. Where you fall on that range depends in large part upon your answers to the following questions:

a. How much of your current income are you saving?

b. How much do you currently spend each year on travel vs. how much you plan to spend on travel once retired?

c. Is your mortgage paid off already? If not, how much is your monthly payment and when will it be paid off?

d. How do you expect your healthcare costs/health insurance to change? Are you retiring prior to being eligible for

Medicare? Do you have long-term care insurance or will you be purchasing it?

e.  Are you supporting anyone else now (e.g. kids or grandkids)? What is the chance you will be supporting/subsidizing loved ones during your retirement?

f.  What new activities/hobbies are planned for retirement (e.g. golf, gambling, fixing up classic cars, etc.) and what are you budgeting for those?

Also, keep in mind that once you have a solid estimate of future expenses, your income requirements need to be adjusted each year to account for inflation. The average inflation rate over the past 30 years has been just under 4%.[1]

3.  <u>Income Sources in Retirement</u>: You need to have an estimate of your Social Security Benefits and Pension (if applicable). Does your pension have a cost of living adjustment? Does your pension continue in full or in part to your spouse after you die?

4.  <u>One Time Cash Inflows or Outflows</u>: Are you going to be selling your residence and adding those funds to your investable assets? Do you plan to pay for a child's wedding? One time inflows or outflows can have a big impact on your retirement plan's probability of success, especially when those inflows or outflows occur early in retirement.

---

1   Source: U.S. Department of Labor Statistics Consumer price Index averages from 1980-2010

5. <u>Other Assumptions</u>: How long you want the money to last. It is common to underestimate how long you will live (as discussed previously). We strongly recommend that you plan for a long life, longer than you think you will realistically live.

Retirement planning involves gathering all of the information above, thinking about how you want to spend your retirement, and then selecting the investments and investment strategy, insurance coverage, and estate planning documents that will give you the highest probability of achieving your financial goals with the least amount of risk.

Let us give you a simplistic rule of thumb since many of you reading this book may not be ready to sit down and develop a detailed plan. Figure out how much you want to spend per year. Let's assume that number is $100,000. Then subtract the amount that will be covered by Social Security, pensions, and other guaranteed income sources. Let's assume that figure is $60,000 per year and it will be increased each year to account for inflation. Therefore, you would need to withdraw the other $40,000 from your investable assets. Most financial planning journals, as well as the AARP, recommend an initial withdrawal rate of only 4%. In our practice, we find that "safe withdrawal rate" is one of the most staggering realizations that most retirees must come to grips with. It was long thought that being a millionaire was financial nirvana. The realization that this $1 million only equates to $40,000 in income is a tough pill for many to swallow. The reason the initial withdrawal rate needs to be so low is so you can increase your income to account for inflation each year without running out of money over the course of a normal retirement (25 years). The low interest rates we are currently witnessing makes generating even $40,000 of income difficult to achieve without taking on some risk. For that reason, it is key to have a well-researched strategy in place before you begin your distributions.

## SOCIAL SECURITY (AT WHAT AGE SHOULD YOU CLAIM BENEFITS?)

Social Security is basically a federally mandated pyramid scheme. Nevertheless, it is the cornerstone of most retirees' "guaranteed" retirement income. Whether Social Security will survive has been an issue of concern and debate for a long time. We think it will absolutely be around. Consider that prior to 1935, when Social Security was first enacted, 50% of our nations seniors lived at or below the poverty level. Today, that figure is closer to 10%. The social fabric of our nation would come apart without Social Security. As a result, Social Security would be one of the last areas of federal spending to be cut. However, it could be "means tested" in the future. For those of you who are not familiar with means testing, it simply means you may not get all of your Social Security benefits if your total income is above a predetermined threshold. If you think that is unlikely, you may be surprised to find out that Medicare has been means tested since 2007. That change was part of the legislation that created the Medicare Part D—prescription drug coverage. In order to pay for prescription drug coverage for all seniors, high income seniors pay more for basic Medicare (Part B). A high income senior still receives Medicare; however, the premium deducted from his or her Social Security check may be as high as $369, whereas most seniors only pay $115 per month (2011 figures). Means testing of benefits is a common budget cutting measure among cash strapped governments. In fact, Greece passed means testing of its Social Security benefits for the first time in 2011 as part of its austerity measures.

Let's assume that Social Security is going to be around in the future in its current form. The big question for most retirees is: Is it better to begin receiving benefits early with a smaller monthly amount, or to wait for a larger monthly payment later? If only there were a simple answer to this question. Unfortunately, the age when you should claim retirement benefits depends on many factors. We are always surprised by how many people (approximately two-thirds) claim benefits as soon as they can (age 62)[2] without any analysis as to whether that is the best decision for their particular situation.

The best wealth maximizing strategy (regarding what age to claim benefits) depends on a number of factors, such as:

- Your current cash needs

- Your health and family longevity

- Whether you plan to work in retirement

- Your other retirement income sources

- Your anticipated future financial needs and obligations

Collecting Social Security as soon as you are eligible is tempting. After all, what if you delay benefits and then you die at age 66? You would never have collected the benefits to which you were entitled.

---

2   Source: http://www.nolo.com/legal-encyclopedia/when-claim-social-security-benefits-29886.html

In addition, many people want the money early in retirement when they are more active and able to travel.

That logic may seem reasonable now. However, the bigger risk is that you will live too long and have insufficient income in your later years. You can claim Social Security any time from age 62-70, but the longer you wait, the larger your monthly check. Many people come out ahead if they wait at least until their full retirement age, which is 66 for people born in the years 1943-1954. Full retirement age slowly increases beyond 66 for people born after 1954.

You will receive about the same amount in lifetime benefits no matter whether you choose to start receiving benefits at age 62, age 70, or any age in between, assuming that you live to the average life expectancy for someone your age. Naturally, if you live longer than your life expectancy, you will receive higher total lifetime payments the longer you wait to begin collecting.

All the number crunching aside, it may be impossible for some households to wait because the breadwinner has lost a job or is no longer able to work. Most financial planners agree that it is smarter to collect earlier if it will prevent you from accumulating debt or depleting a high percentage of your savings.

On the other hand, if you can afford to wait and you are in good health, you should think of the payments you are not receiving as being similar to buying an annuity. This annuity will pay you more inflation-adjusted lifetime income than any annuity you could buy on your own (and is more secure).

Deciding when to collect is easier for a single person because he does not have to worry about how his decision will affect a spouse. It usually pays to wait until your full retirement age if you can support yourself until then and you are in decent health. It may make sense to wait until age 70, for people with significant savings who expect to live well into their 80s or beyond.

Planning for married couples is more complex because there are age differences, varying retirement dates, varying lifetime earnings records, and other factors to consider. In many cases, the higher-earning spouse should delay his or her benefits until age 70, while the lower earner begins to collect at age 62. That way, when one spouse dies, the survivor collects the higher of his or her own benefit or the benefit his or her spouse was collecting (or entitled to collect). This strategy ensures that the surviving spouse will end up with the maximum amount of benefits for the rest of his or her life.

## Spousal Benefits

Each person will get a Social Security retirement benefit based on either his own work record or half of his spouse's benefit (whichever is greater). You can apply for your Social Security benefit based on your own work record once you are 62, but you cannot claim a spousal benefit until your spouse reaches his or her full retirement age and files for his or her benefits.

## File & Suspend

What if you want to wait until age 70 to collect benefits, but your spouse wants to claim a spousal benefit on your work record before then? You can file for benefits at your Full Retirement Age (66) but immediately suspend them before ever receiving a payment. This clever strategy, called "File & Suspend," enables the lower-earning spouse to get up to half of the higher earner's benefits, while the higher earner's benefits continue to accrue. It enables the married couple, where one spouse's earnings record is significantly lower than the other's, to get the most out of the system. It gives the couple some cash flow now while accruing the highest possible payment for the higher earning spouse and eventually for the surviving spouse. From a financial planning perspective, you want the last survivor to have the highest possible payment.

Here's a question: If the couple can afford it, should the lower earning spouse also wait until full retirement age or later? That only makes sense if you are confident that both spouses will live well into their 80s and you don't need the income now.

## Switching Benefits

Married couples with similar lifetime earnings may also consider another strategy. Here, one person claims spousal benefits at full retirement age and switches to his or her own, and presumably higher, benefits later. That's right; you can claim a spousal benefit at age 66 and your own benefit will continue to increase at 8% per year from age 66 to age 70. You would switch to the benefits based on your own record at age 70.

## FAQ's about Social Security

### Can I collect benefits even if I continue working?

You can earn as much as you want without affecting your Social Security benefits once you reach your full retirement age. However, between age 62 and your full retirement age, you can only earn up to the "Earnings Threshold" which is currently $14,160. For every $2 you earn above the threshold, your benefits will be reduced by $1. However, no need to despair. If Social Security withholds some of your benefits because you continue to work, it will pay you a higher monthly benefit amount when you reach your full retirement age. In other words, if you would like to work and earn more than the exempt amount, you should know that it will not, on average, reduce the total value of your lifetime benefits. In fact, working after you begin collecting Social Security may actually increase your lifetime benefits.

### How much will my payments be reduced for claiming retirement benefits early?

Benefits are reduced by approximately 0.52% for every month you collect benefits before your full retirement age. If your monthly benefit would be $1,000 a month at your full retirement age of 66, you will collect only $750 per month if you claim benefits at age 62.

### Are spousal benefits also reduced by the same amount for claiming early?

No. Claiming Social Security at age 62 reduces your monthly benefit by 25%. If you are claiming benefits (at age 62) based on your spouse's work record, your benefits will be reduced by 30% (this assumes your full retirement age is 66).

### How much are benefits increased if I delay retirement benefits to age 70?

You accrue "Delayed Retirement Credits," which increase your benefits at a rate of 2/3rds of 1% for every month (8% per year) you wait beyond your full retirement age.

### If I get married, am I immediately entitled to spousal benefits?

You have to be married for one year before you are entitled to spousal benefits.

### What if my spouse died prior to collecting benefits?

You have to have been married for nine months in order to collect spousal survivor benefits and you have to wait until you are at least 60 years old to begin collecting (unless accidental death).

### What happens to spousal benefits in the case of divorce?

If you were married for 10 years and are not currently remarried, you can claim benefits on your prior spouse's record. In this day and age, it is not uncommon for two or three people to be claiming spousal benefits on one person's work record.

### Can I pay back the benefits I collected between ages 62-70 and then get a higher payment as if I had never collected?

No. You used to be able to do so. Lots of financial advisors talked about this possibility, but few people actually did it. In any case, this option was eliminated in 2010.

### Are the ages at which you qualify for benefits the same for widows or divorcees?

Widows (or surviving divorced spouses) can claim survivor benefits at age 60. Divorcees can qualify for benefits at age 62 even if the ex-spouse (age 62 or older) has not filed yet for benefits. Note: you have to have been divorced for at least two years prior to filing for spousal benefits on an ex-spouse's record.

**What is the Full Retirement Age for people born after 1954?**

| Year of Birth | Full Retirement Age |
| --- | --- |
| 1943-1954 | 66 |
| 1955 | 66 and 2 months |
| 1956 | 66 and 4 months |
| 1957 | 66 and 6 months |
| 1958 | 66 and 8 months |
| 1959 | 66 and 10 months |
| 1960 and later | 67 |

## PENSIONS (LUMP SUM VS. PAYMENTS, SINGLE LIFE VS. JOINT LIFE)

*"Why is there so much month left at the end of the money?"*
— John Barrymore

Like most decisions in financial planning, there are no absolutes when it comes to pension decisions. The correct (pension election) decision depends on your personal circumstances (primarily your age, income needs, and the health of you and your spouse).

**When you retire, if you have a traditional pension (defined benefit), you need to make an important pension decision either to:**

1. Roll over the entire lump sum to an IRA and invest it however you see fit.

2. Take a payout of lifetime income.

You can skip the rest of this section if you have already decided to roll over your lump sum to an IRA.

**If you have decided to select lifetime income, you have a second decision to make, either to choose:**

1. Life Only: This option gives you the highest monthly payment for your lifetime but does not continue to your spouse after your death.

2. Joint & Survivor: This option has a lower payment but continues on for the surviving spouse (sometimes at a reduced level such as 50% or 66%).

Many married couples quickly decide on the Joint & Survivor option. After all, many people still like their spouses and do not want to leave them in dire straits. The Joint & Survivor option seems like the safe way to go. The downside, of course, is that you have a lower payment for your entire retirement, and if you outlive your spouse, this choice turns out to have been the wrong decision (for maximizing wealth). An alternative exists, which is known by some in the industry as Pension Max.

## Pension Max

Pension Max is a strategy where you elect the Life Only option, which gives you the highest payment. You then take the difference between the Life Only payment (let's say that is $4,000) and the Joint & Survivor option (let's say that is $3,000), and you use the $1,000 difference to buy life insurance on your life. If you die first, then your pension payment stops, but your spouse would have the death benefit from the life insurance to replace the lost income. However, if you outlive your spouse, you could cash out the life insurance and enjoy the higher monthly income for the rest of your life. Alternatively, you could continue paying the life insurance premiums and leave a nice tax-free death benefit to your heirs.

Let's continue our example from above in the context of a husband and wife who are both age 65. For them, $1,000 per month would buy approximately $460,000 of death benefit on a permanent life policy, level payments, with a no-lapse guarantee for a male (standard rate class, non-smoker). If the husband were to die first at age 82, the death benefit could be used to buy an immediate annuity that would provide $4,451 per month for life for an 82 year-old female. Naturally, the surviving spouse (the wife in this example) does not need to buy an annuity, but she has the option to use the lump sum however she sees fit. The immediate annuity makes sense if she is in good health and needs the income. If she is in poor health and/or doesn't need the income, she can put the money in the bank and take withdrawals if/when needed.

The scenario where this option really maximizes wealth is if the wife were to pass away first. We are not hoping for this situation, but it does happen 20% of the time (for spouses who are the same age), according to the U.S. Census Bureau. In this case, the death benefit is a pure increase in the value of your estate for your heirs. Alternatively, you can surrender the life insurance policy, keep the cash value (if any), and retain the higher monthly income ($1,000 a month in this example) for the rest of your life.

## ANNUITIES

When people retire, they need to determine how they are going to fund their lifestyles for the rest of their lives. Some retirees have one or more pensions that, combined with Social Security, meet all of their income needs. Income planning is pretty simple if you are fortunate enough to be in this situation. However, most people need to supplement their "guaranteed" income sources with savings and investments. The first major decision is whether you want to *transfer* the investment risk, longevity risk, and interest rate risk to an insurance company for a fee. This arrangement is called an annuity. The alternative to buying annuities is to manage your investments in such a way that they provide a steady stream of income over the rest of your life. Both options for creating a lifetime income stream—annuities and traditional investment portfolios—are described in detail over the next few pages.

In a widely cited study, Wharton Business School professor David Babbel concluded that a retiree who didn't annuitize some savings would need a nest egg 25-40% larger than people with annuities in their portfolio. The "Babbel study" was commissioned by members of the insurance industry, but it has swayed some skeptics.

Another recent boost to those in favor of annuities came in the form of a Government Accountability Office (GAO) report that was released July 1, 2011. The GAO was asked by Senator Herb Kohl of Wisconsin, who is the chairman of the Special Committee on Aging, to report on the best way to ensure that retirees have money to last the rest of their lives. He asked the GAO what the experts recommend to retirees, what those retirees actually do, and what policy decisions could be implemented to ensure that retirees don't run out of money for their basic living expenses. The report entitled: *Retirement Income: Ensuring Income throughout Retirement Requires Difficult Choices,* suggested that delaying Social Security and purchasing an income annuity may be the only way to ensure solvency in retirement.

An annuity is the only product that guarantees lifetime income backed by the claims-paying ability of large insurance companies. Annuities are among the most misunderstood of all investment vehicles. Many of the misconceptions are based on outdated viewpoints that do not take into consideration the tremendous advances in product design. Allianz Life Insurance Company hired two independent research firms to study consumer opinions on annuities. The study surveyed 3,257 people during the month of May 2010. Here are some of the findings of that study[3], which had a margin of error of +/-1.7%:

- 54% of respondents expressed distaste for the word "annuity," even after describing an "annuity like" solution.

- 25% of respondents formed their opinions on annuities more than 20 years ago and another 28% said that they formed their opinion between 10-20 years ago.

- 76% of annuity owners surveyed were happy with their annuities.

---

3   Source: Allianz. White Paper: "Reclaiming the Future." Larson Research and Strategy Consulting, and DSS Research." (May 2010): 2-16.

- Consumers ranked annuities second-highest in satisfaction among all financial instruments beating out mutual funds, stocks, bonds, and CDs.

An interesting footnote to the survey is that gold and precious metals ranked first in investor satisfaction. This preference is a textbook example of many of the psychological biases we have discussed in this book. Precious metals had been enjoying a tremendous run up in price at the time of the survey. Participants in the survey clearly indicated that they prefer safety, even if it means lower returns, vs. more volatile investments that have the chance for higher returns. Precious metals historically have been susceptible to dramatic booms and busts. It seems as though the investors in the survey were exhibiting recency bias, extrapolation bias, and overconfidence.

Annuities have many great features and also a whole host of issues that need to be understood. More than anything, annuities suffer from an image problem in the minds of many consumers and in the press. Some annuity features that clients did not like have been eliminated. For example, most of the annuity products today do not require annuity owners to "annuitize" their policy in order to get guaranteed lifetime income. "Annuitization" means that you make an irrevocable decision to convert your account value into a stream of payments (for life). Many people do not want to annuitize because it eliminates any future flexibility regarding the amount and timing of withdrawals. It also usually means no death benefit is left to your heirs. Annuity owners can receive less money than they originally invested if they annuitize and then die prematurely. Annuity owners felt they were taking a gamble where they needed to live a certain number of years in order to "break even."

## A New Generation of Guarantees

The newer annuity policies typically have Guaranteed Minimum Withdrawal Benefits (GMWB) or Guaranteed Minimum Income Benefits (GMIB). These features guarantee income for the lives of one or both spouses *without annuitizing* the contract. Each withdrawal is simply being subtracted from the policy's account value. In this scenario, there is typically still a death benefit equal to the remaining account value, as long as the contract value is not depleted during the owner's lifetime. If the account value is depleted (i.e. you run out of money), then the insurance company is required to continue making the monthly payments for the remainder of your life. In essence, you are transferring the risk of running out of money to the insurance company.

Many contracts also have enhanced death benefit riders that increase the death benefit each year by a predetermined percentage, regardless of any increase in the actual account values. Therefore, annuities typically are guaranteeing lifetime income, a minimum death benefit, or some combination of both. These guarantees can reduce the behavioral biases of "retail investors." In other words, the guarantees give investors the comfort and confidence to stay the course during uncertain economic times.

It should be pointed out that these new guarantees are typically riders (or optional benefits) that may not be included in the basic annuity contract. The riders may have additional fees or charges that need to be considered when evaluating a given annuity.

## Confessions of a Variable Annuity Critic

In the mid-1990s, Moshe A. Milevsky, Ph.D., a finance professor at York University in Toronto, and Dr. Steven Posner, who was then working as a derivatives analyst for Goldman Sachs, researched and published a study on the costs and benefits of variable annuities. They analyzed over 400 variable annuity policies and compared the fees being charged to their "theoretical value." These so-called theoretical values were intended to represent the cost of replacing the guarantees using derivatives (NOTE: a derivative is a contract between two parties that specifies conditions under which payments, or payoffs, are to be made between the parties). Their primary motivation was academic and intellectual curiosity regarding whether consumers were getting their money's worth. Their conclusion was that purchasers of annuities were being grossly overcharged. The guarantees at that time were typically death benefit guarantees that simply provided a "Return of Premium" on death. That meant that if you invested $100,000 and your contract declined to $70,000 (assuming no withdrawals) then the death benefit would still be $100,000. Very few annuities at the time had Guaranteed Minimum Income/Withdrawal Benefits and/or Enhanced Death Benefits.

These findings—which were eventually published after scientific review in the prestigious *Journal of Risk and Insurance* in 2001 and subsequently quoted numerous times in publications ranging from *The Wall Street Journal* to *Reader's Digest*—were seized upon by investor advocates, financial commentators, regulators, and plaintiff lawyers as evidence that variable annuities were overpriced, oversold, and unsuitable.

Professor Milevsky never said that variable annuities were evil, dangerous, or unsuitable. His basic position was that, for many investors, a similar financial outcome could be achieved at a lower cost.

However, in 2007 he updated his research and wrote:

> I am seeing an enormous shift in the way variable annuity policies are being designed, priced and marketed to the public. It is now time for me to update my official position on these instruments.
>
> In fact, after spending quite a bit of time poring over some of the more recent designs as well as talking to actuaries, regulators and advisors, I'm not even sure these instruments deserve the old (and maligned) name of variable annuities.
>
> This isn't your grandmother's variable annuity!
>
> Regardless of what you want to call these increasingly heterogeneous products, it seems the relative value pendulum has swung in the opposite direction. I can no longer claim that you are being overcharged for these guarantees or that you can achieve similar goals at a lower cost. It would be very difficult and expensive to bake a living benefit in your kitchen....
>
> Indeed, when you take into account the new living benefit riders such as guaranteed minimum withdrawal benefits (GMWBs),

guaranteed minimum accumulation benefits (GMABs) and guaranteed minimum income benefits (GMIBs), these products (a blend of finance and insurance) are creating a different type of protection. They protect the owner in the event that something goes awfully wrong during the early part of their retirement or when they start generating income. And, after the market meltdown earlier this decade, this so-called "sequence of returns" risk might not seem as remote as during the euphoria of the late '90s. Indeed, markets don't have to go down and stay down to ruin your retirement. All you need is a bear market at the wrong time, and the sustainability of your income can be cut in half.

This leads me to my main point, which is that I'm now getting exceedingly worried that some insurance companies are not charging enough....

Yes, this sounds like an odd thing to say given the position of my earlier study....

As an example, a colleague of mine, Dr. Thomas Salisbury, and I recently published a study in the actuarial journal Insurance: Mathematics and Economics in 2006 demonstrating that the GMWB rider, which charges an extra 30 to 50 basis points, might actually cost between 75 and 160 basis points to hedge in the capital markets.[4] And that number does not even include any insurance company profit margins, commissions and transaction costs.

---

4   NOTE: 100 basis points = 1%

Professor Milevsky's concern when he published his revised opinion was that insurance companies may not be charging enough, so you should carefully consider the financial strength of the insurer as part of your evaluation process. Many insurers have reduced their guarantees on new policies and raised the costs of some riders over the past few years. Suffice it to say, the marketplace is rapidly changing faster than George Clooney changes girlfriends. In fact, the two annuity products we liked the best (last year) for guaranteeing future income are no longer available. However, new products were introduced this year that we believe currently have the best lifetime income guarantees.

## The Downside to Annuities

When you buy an annuity, you are transferring risk to an insurance company for a fee just like you do with other types of insurance (auto, home, liability, etc.) You have to decide whether the fees and restrictions are worth the peace of mind you would have knowing that you will have a guaranteed income for life. Annuity products are complicated, and unfortunately, they do not lend themselves very well to side-by-side comparisons. Furthermore, the prospectuses and offering documents make the IRS tax code look like light reading. So you need to do your homework and work with a financial advisor you trust.

Annuities are not right for every investor, every situation, or for all of your money (recall our discussion about diversification). In fact, we attribute a large part of annuities' "image problem" to the fact that they are sometimes oversold. Many financial advisors present themselves as "planners," but in reality, they are simply annuity salespeople. You know what they say, "If the only tool you have is a hammer, every problem looks like a nail." We recommend that you work with a financial advisor who is well-versed in annuities but also equally comfortable designing a more traditional investment portfolio that is geared toward income.

## INVESTING FOR INCOME

You can use a traditional investment portfolio to accomplish the same objectives as intended with annuities. An investment portfolio, which we refer to as a "managed account," typically has lower fees than an annuity, more flexibility, and may be better suited for an inflationary environment. The managed account just lacks the insurance company "guarantees" provided by the annuity. If you plan to create inflation-adjusted income from your investment portfolio you need to understand a few things:

The two phases of your financial life are:

- The **Accumulation Phase**, where you are saving and investing for retirement.

- The **Distribution Phase**, when you are using your accumulated savings to supplement your retirement income.

To maximize your financial security, the manner in which you manage your investments should be dramatically different during these two phases. The importance of this shift in investing strategy is often misunderstood by retirees. Many assume that the key difference is that retirees simply need to invest more conservatively since they cannot afford big losses. In reality, there is more to it than that.

Consider this scenario: Two investors each average a 9% rate of return over a 25-year period during the **Accumulation Phase** of their financial lives. The only difference between these two investors is the sequence of returns. Investor #1 had good years in the beginning and poor results at the end. Investor #2 had the opposite sequence of returns, poor results in the beginning and good returns at the end. (Remember that they both averaged a 9% rate of return over the 25-year period.) Who ends up with more money? The answer is they will have exactly the same. Performance is typically measured by return on investment, during the accumulation phase.

However, what if these investors were now retired, in the **Distribution Phase** of their financial lives, and taking a 5% withdrawal each year and increasing their withdrawal each year for inflation? Do they each still have the same amount of money at the end of 25 years? The answer to that question is a big **NO!**

Investor #1, who had the good years early, may have 2-3 times what he started with after 25 years of distributions. However, Investor #2 with the poor investment results in early years is likely to be out of money. Why is that? The sequence of returns matters when you are taking distributions. In fact, when you are taking regular distributions from your portfolio, the proper performance measure is no longer your annual return on investment. It is "consistency and sustainability of income." Consider the following example[5]:

**1 Feast:** Consider an investor who was fortunate enough to invest $1 million in S&P 500 Index on January 1, 1983. He takes a withdrawal of $75,000 the first year, and increases his withdrawals by 3% each subsequent year to adjust for inflation. How would this investor have fared over 20 years?

**2 Famine:** Consider the same scenario, except we'll completely reverse the order of the returns so that 2002 comes first and 1983 comes last. Instead of taking more than $2 million in withdrawals, the investor would have taken under $1.7 million. More importantly, the investor would have run out of money in less than 17 years!

| Year | Market Performance | Investment Balance | Withdrawl |
|------|------|------|------|
| 1983 | 22.51% | 1,000,000 | 75,000 |
| 1984 | 6.27% | 1,141,659 | 77,250 |
| 1985 | 32.16% | 1,133,569 | 79,568 |
| 1986 | 18.47% | 1,405,763 | 81,955 |
| 1987 | 5.23% | 1,575,884 | 84,413 |
| 1988 | 16.81% | 1,571,682 | 86,946 |
| 1989 | 31.49% | 1,741,629 | 89,554 |
| 1990 | -3.17% | 2,186,414 | 92,241 |
| 1991 | 30.55% | 2,026,326 | 95,008 |
| 1992 | 7.67% | 2,535,848 | 97,858 |
| 1993 | 9.99% | 2,628,737 | 100,794 |
| 1994 | 1.31% | 2,785,519 | 103,818 |
| 1995 | 37.43% | 2,717,512 | 106,932 |
| 1996 | 23.07% | 3,607,732 | 110,140 |
| 1997 | 33.36% | 4,317,191 | 113,444 |
| 1998 | 26.58% | 5,625,040 | 116,848 |
| 1999 | 21.04% | 7,099,131 | 120,353 |
| 2000 | -9.11% | 8,459,774 | 123,964 |
| 2001 | -11.88% | 7,570,771 | 127,682 |
| 2002 | -22.10% | 6,551,266 | 131,513 |
| Ending Value | | 4,986,455 | 2,015,278 |

| Year | Market Performance | Investment Balance | Withdrawl |
|------|------|------|------|
| 2002 | -22.10% | 1,000,000 | 75,000 |
| 2001 | -11.88% | 712,288 | 77,250 |
| 2000 | -9.11% | 555,006 | 79,568 |
| 1999 | 21.04% | 428,502 | 81,955 |
| 1998 | 28.58% | 428,083 | 84,413 |
| 1997 | 33.36% | 456,953 | 86,946 |
| 1996 | 23.07% | 503,944 | 89,554 |
| 1995 | 37.43% | 520,320 | 92,241 |
| 1994 | 1.31% | 605,572 | 95,008 |
| 1993 | 9.99% | 517,875 | 97,858 |
| 1992 | 7.67% | 466,865 | 100,794 |
| 1991 | 30.55% | 398,014 | 103,818 |
| 1990 | -3.17% | 399,931 | 106,932 |
| 1989 | 31.49% | 282,016 | 110,140 |
| 1988 | 16.81% | 243,342 | 113,444 |
| 1987 | 5.23% | 161,268 | 116,848 |
| 1986 | 18.47% | 49,800 | 120,353 |
| 1985 | 32.16% | -70,553 | 123,964 |
| 1984 | 6.27% | 0 | 0 |
| 1983 | 22.51% | 0 | 0 |
| Ending Value | | 0 | 1,691,108 |

You can't control the sequence of returns, but you can manage your money differently so that poor investment performance in the early years of your retirement does not ruin your retirement plan. We will

5    Taken from Prudential Annuities brochure #IFS-A163932. August, 2009.

explain how in a minute, but first, let's get a better understanding of the problem.

## The Problem

The #1 financial goal of most retirees is to generate enough retirement income to live comfortably, increase that income each year to keep pace with inflation, and ensure that they do not outlive their money. This task is not easy when you consider that many people will be retired and active for 20-40 years.

Studies show that many retirees have unrealistic expectations about money. For example, many retirees overestimate how much money they can safely withdraw from their portfolios each year and underestimate their life expectancies and the impact of inflation.

## The Three Common Mistakes Retirees Make:

1) Thinking an **extremely conservative approach** to investing (CDs and bonds) is the safest way to ensure they do not run out of money. The reality is that this approach will not support a long retirement because these investments do not have the growth potential to replace withdrawals and keep pace with inflation.

2) Trying to **live only on interest and dividends** without touching the principal. This strategy may work for a while. However, consider that with a 3% inflation rate, $5,000 worth of purchases today will cost you $7,790 fifteen years from now. Also, consider that interest rates are not stable or predictable. What if you retired in the early 1980s and based your retirement plan on the then prevailing interest rate of 10%, but now you are trying to live on interest rates of 2-5%.

Your retirement income will have to be dramatically reduced if you follow this approach.

3) Building a **portfolio of stocks and bonds and then taking systematic withdrawals** proportionately from each of the investments. In 2007, Morningstar Inc. published a research study (see chart below) that showed the probability of running out of money for various investment portfolios (conservative to aggressive) and various withdrawal rates (4-8%). For example, consider an initial withdrawal rate of 6% of the starting portfolio balance; each year your withdrawal would be increased to keep pace with inflation. If you had 100% of your portfolio invested in bonds, you would have only a 3% likelihood of your retirement account lasting for 25 years. Your probability of success shoots up to 69% with a 100% stock portfolio.[6]

## Probability of Not Totally Depleting
## Your Retirement Portfolio in 25 Years

Conservative ———————————————————————— Aggressive

| Withdrawal Rate | 100% Bonds | 50% Bonds/ 50% Stocks | 100% Stocks |
|---|---|---|---|
| 4% | 83% | 96% | 92% |
| 6% | 3% | 57% | 69% |
| 8% | 0% | 13% | 41% |

Most retirees would not be comfortable with only a 69% probability of not outliving their money. Additionally, most retirees would not be comfortable having all of their investable assets in the stock

6   Assumed inflation rate is 3.1%; assumed investment expenses are .94% for stock mutual funds and .82% for bond funds. Analysis ignores taxes and transaction costs.

market. Therefore, most financial literature and advisors recommend a lower initial withdrawal rate, such as 4%, to improve your chances. Naturally, if you only need 1-3%, you can make a lot of mistakes and still not run out. If you need 4-6%, that is a different story.

## The Solution

So, what is the best investment strategy to provide maximum retirement income through good times and bad without depleting your portfolio? The answer to this question has been the subject of considerable research.

In our practice, we use a strategy to produce retirement income that has been shown to produce a higher income stream, provide a higher probability of not outliving your money, and frequently have a higher ending portfolio value. We call this strategy: **Income Harvesting**.[7] We have found the results produced by Income Harvesting to be superior to all competing investment strategies we have analyzed. The strategy matches short-term needs with short-term cash availability and long-term needs with higher yielding, long-term investments. An overview of the Income Harvesting model follows on the next couple of pages. However, this discussion is not an in-depth instruction manual on how to implement this strategy. That is beyond the scope of this book, and frankly, it is probably beyond the capabilities of most do-it-yourself investors. If you would like to follow the same concepts while managing your own retirement income portfolio, we suggest you read the book *The Buckets of Money Retirement Solution* by Ray Lucia.

---

7   Source: "Income Harvesting" strategy is based on a 2007 Judges Grant winner in the Financial Frontiers Competition. Results published in the *Journal of Financial Planning* (Aug 2008) by Zachary S. Parker, CFP, LUTCF.

The research for our Income Harvesting Strategy is based on back-tested data that analyzed its success in maintaining inflation adjusted income over a 25-year period. In 100% of the 25-year periods between 1931 and 2004, the strategy was successful even when annual distributions began at 6% of the portfolio value and increased by 3% per year for inflation. In addition, the ending portfolio balance was at least *double* what the client started with in 98% of those 25-year periods.

The only time the strategy did not support that level of income were those 25-year periods that began between 1927 and 1930. As with all investment strategies, past performance is no guarantee of future results.

This Income Harvesting strategy requires that your Retirement Portfolio be divided into four different accounts:

**Account #1: income-guaranteed account.** This account contains cash equivalents and a laddered bond portfolio. This account is used to provide a substantial period of guaranteed income. All withdrawals are paid out of this account.

**Accounts #2 and #3: investment accounts.** These accounts contain well-diversified portfolios that include international and domestic stocks in large and small companies as well as real estate and alternative asset classes. These accounts provide the growth to replenish Account #1 and to sustain the overall portfolio for 25 or more years. Some people will question why you need two different investment accounts, which may have the exact same investments in them. The two accounts play different roles in the overall strategy and are subject to different "Decision Rules" that dictate when certain actions are taken.

**Account #4: an ultra-safe account.** This account is the glue to the strategy. It can only contain investments where the principal is guaranteed and the maturity is one year or less (e.g. CDs). Account #4 provides "portfolio insurance" for major market downturns by essentially sitting on the sidelines until a market downturn of 30% or more, at which time it gets added to the investment accounts. You might be interested to know that we have had a 30% downturn in the broad U.S. stock market 13 times over the last 65 years (1946-2011).

The dramatically better results of this Income Harvesting strategy vs. competing income distribution models are largely attributable to the Decision Rules that dictate which investments get liquidated and in what proportion each year. Most retirement investing strategies take systematic withdrawals, which come equally from all of the investments, or the withdrawals always come from the same place, ignoring the prior year's market performance.

The Decision Rules eliminate emotional decision-making and many of the psychological biases discussed earlier in the book (i.e. overconfidence, extrapolation bias, disposition effect, etc.). They also guide the investor to buy after the market declines and sell after the market rallies. The Income Harvesting strategy is flexible enough to accommodate a range of risk tolerances from conservative to aggressive, a range of retirement time horizons, and a corresponding range of desired withdrawal rates.

For many people, a fully liquid strategy such as this one, combined with some guaranteed income sources found in quality annuity products, is a powerful solution to meeting their retirement income needs. Each person must find the proper balance of liquidity and guarantees for his or her personal situation.

# CHAPTER 6

# LEGACY PLANNING

---

*"The measure of who we are is what we do with what we have..."*
— Vince Lombardi

You can only do two things with money: 1) Spend it, or 2) Save it for the future. Eventually your future will come to an end and anything that you did not spend will be passed on to someone else. We have found that retirees differ greatly in terms of their desire to leave something to the next generation. In general, a consensus exists among the retirees with whom we  meet that their top priority is to have enough income for the rest of their lives. Once that goal is met, many retirees really love the idea of helping their kids and/or grandkids and/or their favorite worthy cause. Although this assistance is typically a secondary goal, some planning in this area can go a long way.

Many people spend so much time earning and saving their money that they don't really think about what happens to it once they pass on. Having had first-hand experience with watching wealth transfer from one generation to the next, we can tell you that good preparation is the key. We all want to believe that little Johnny or Sally is going to be a good steward of our life's work. However, unarmed and ill-prepared, many adult children end up with results similar to the horror stories we hear of lottery winners.

## BENEFICIARIES—CAN YOU CONTROL WHAT THEY DO?

*"I'm not young enough to know everything."*
— Oscar Wilde

Let's face it—all beneficiaries are not created equal. Some are very responsible while others will blow everything faster than a grandmother can pull a baby picture from her purse. The other issue is that even responsible beneficiaries may make bad investment choices if they have never had discretion over a large chunk of money. Just imagine if a young person inherited a large amount of money in the late '90s. He very well may have put it all into Internet stocks and lost it all. If he inherited it in the mid-2000s, he may have put it all into residential real estate and seen all his equity disappear almost overnight. The bottom line is that most people learn about investing through trial and error. Hopefully, you make your mistakes when you are young and the errors are not catastrophic. Unfortunately, beneficiaries of large sums of money frequently learn very expensive lessons with your life savings and don't get a "do over."

In our practice, we have seen our clients' children blow through large inheritances in short order. In one case, we witnessed a woman go from inheriting millions to seeking government assistance within two years. The primary reason was that when her parents were alive, they rationed the money to help sustain her in times of need. Once her parents were gone, she was left to her own devices. She spent uncontrollably, and against our advice (and with absolutely no experience), she started her own restaurant. The restaurant failed after only five months, leaving her without a dime. Worse than that, she was sued by her creditors, had to file for bankruptcy, and seek government assistance just to cover her basic needs. The saddest part is that this entire situation could have been avoided with proper planning that included a trust, which would have distributed limited amounts of money over time.

Another estate planning problem is the pesky son or daughter-in-law whom you don't like. What if your child's marriage ends in divorce? You don't want half of the money you left to your adorable child going to your evil "soon-to-be" ex-son/daughter-in-law. So what can you do? Here are the best solutions:

1. Leave a Letter of Instruction ("What if" Letter): This is the simplest thing to do, but keep in mind that your letter of instruction is simply an expression of your wishes. It is not legally binding and your beneficiaries can choose to ignore it. However, at least you get a chance to communicate your hopes and values. We recommend that you keep all of your estate planning documents and your letter of instruction in a specific drawer or file cabinet and communicate that location to whoever is going to inherit or manage the estate after you pass on.

   One of our clients left a letter of instruction for his daughter that told her to keep the money she would inherit in a separate account (in her name only) and not to comingle it with her husband's assets or general family assets. This client is not too fond of his son-in-law, to put it mildly. Since this client lived in a community property state, the inheritance would not usually be part of any divorce settlement as long as it was never co-mingled. Other examples of things that could be put in a letter of instruction include requesting that the money left be used to pay for education, family vacations, to purchase a home, to pay for a wedding, and more.

2. <u>Put Incentive Language in the Beneficiary Section of your Estate Planning Documents</u>: Most people will have either a Will or a Revocable Living Trust that designates who gets which assets when you pass on. A Will is more likely to be contested, and the assets have to go through a legal process called probate, which can be time-consuming and expensive for your beneficiaries. Therefore, a trust is typically recommended for anyone with any significant assets and/or challenging family situations (i.e. second marriages or problem beneficiaries).

Once you pass away, the person who is responsible for administering your trust (the successor trustee) or your Will (the executor/executrix) must carry out your instructions. Remember that your Will and/or your Revocable Living Trust becomes irrevocable when you (and in most cases, your spouse) die.

Another situation where a trust is more useful than a Will is if you want to provide incentives meant to encourage or discourage certain behaviors of your beneficiary(s). You cannot include incentive language in a Will. Trust provisions, on the other hand, can be very effective in controlling inheritances. Instead of leaving your wealth in one lump sum to a child, you can place certain restrictions that determine when and how the money gets distributed. Some requirements that people use are age of distribution, distribution over a period of years, employment, graduation from college, passing a drug test, etc. There are very few things that you cannot specify as conditions for receiving an inheritance. (Among those very few are that you cannot require that your children get a divorce or marry someone of the same race or religion as conditions of receiving their inheritance.) Incentive language effectively motivates the beneficiary to mature and live a responsible life in order to gain access to his or her inheritance.

Keep in mind that if the restrictions in the trust are too hindering or too numerous, the trust could become unrealistic, causing resentment and further rebellion. Additionally, many would argue that incentive provisions are an attempt to control children from the grave and are a final (and possibly futile) attempt at imparting values you were not able to impart during your lifetime. If an incentive trust is worded improperly, it could overlook the child's actual needs, such as his or her overall health and medical needs. So, make sure you also place an emergency and special needs safety net into the trust. Use phrasing such as the HEMS provision: "This trust is intended for the health, education, maintenance, and support of my child."

3. <u>Create a Spendthrift Trust</u>: A revocable trust that contains the provisions mentioned previously, which control the conditions upon which money gets distributed, is essentially a "spendthrift trust." A spendthrift trust is an irrevocable trust that puts restrictions on withdrawals. For example, you can give the beneficiary a monthly allowance and/or periodic lump sum payments for life or until the funds are fully disbursed. Spendthrift trusts sometimes contain provisions giving the trustee discretion to distribute money ahead of schedule but only for specific purposes such as education, medical expenses, or other necessities, but not for fancy cars, luxury vacations, or extravagant parties. Thus, it is important that you choose trustees who are not likely to be influenced by your beneficiaries.

A properly constructed spendthrift trust protects the proceeds you leave the beneficiary from possible claims by his or her creditors or divorcing spouses. In general, creditors cannot access any of the spendthrift trust assets until they are distributed to the beneficiaries.

A less elaborate alternative to creating a spendthrift trust might be to purchase an annuity or have your trust purchase an annuity upon your death, with the payments going to your chosen beneficiary for his or her lifetime or for a fixed period such as 20 years. Some states even exempt unlimited annuity payments and life insurance proceeds from the claims of creditors. The annuity's guaranteed income stream helps ensure some measure of financial security for the beneficiary. So long as the beneficiary is not made the owner of the annuity, he or she is not readily able to convert that long-term income stream into a lump sum.

Another consideration to keep in mind is the time, effort, and money that will be required to carry out the provisions in your trust. It is pretty easy to distribute the assets right away. However, if the assets are going to be distributed over time, an ongoing commitment will be required from your successor trustee. After your death, your trust will have to file its own tax return and any income earned by the trust, which is not distributed, will be taxed at the trust's tax rate (frequently higher than the beneficiary's tax rate). You can also name an independent third party trustee if you do not have a good candidate to manage the trust after your death. Most large banks have trustee services, and there are also trust companies locally and nationwide. Third party trustees typically charge in the neighborhood of 1% of the assets in the trust.

## LIFE INSURANCE AS A WEALTH TRANSFER TOOL

*"I made my money the old fashioned way. I was very nice to a wealthy relative right before he died."*
— Malcolm Forbes

Most people think of life insurance as a way to protect their family (replace lost wages) in the case of a premature death. Cash value life insurance is also frequently used as a way to save for and eventually fund retirement. Both are excellent uses

for life insurance and valuable tools for the right situations. However, we are not going to talk about either of those uses for life insurance in this book. We want to discuss the use of life insurance as a tool to transfer wealth to the next generation.

Many seniors quickly dismiss life insurance as something they no longer need. That may be true, especially if it's likely that they will need all of their assets to support their lifestyle in retirement. However, many seniors have more assets than they will ever spend and are planning to leave money to the next generation and/or charities. You should take a second look at life insurance if you are confident you are never going to spend all of your money.

**Four Important Points about Life Insurance:**

1. Life insurance is cheaper and more efficient than it has ever been. You can buy more death benefit for less money than you could 10 years ago.

2. You cannot beat the tax treatment of life insurance: tax-free.

3. It's pretty tough to screw it up. In other words, in the beginning of this book we covered a variety of psychological biases that lead the "retail investor" to make bad financial decisions. However, once you own the life insurance, not a lot of decisions need to be made. Pay the premium and you have a guaranteed death benefit. There is nothing to manage.

4. There is not a single asset that is more desirable to inherit.

Read the following two examples to get a better understanding of how our clients have used life insurance as a wealth transfer tool.

## Life Insurance: Example #1

We recently placed a policy for a single 72-year-old female client. She does not presently have an estate tax problem. Her total net worth is about $1.2 million, with approximately $900,000 as investable assets (i.e. non-real estate). She is a very conservative investor who has enough income and takes minimal withdrawals from her portfolio (<1% per year). Her home is paid for, and she already has long-term care insurance. She plans to leave most of the money to her son.

She is in excellent health and qualified for a preferred plus rate class. She chose to fund the life insurance with annuities and CDs that will be maturing over the next seven years. Therefore, we set up the premium payment schedule as a seven-pay, meaning she will make seven annual payments of $25,000 each. After seven years, the policy will be "paid up" and she will never make another payment. The most she would possibly pay into the policy is $175,000 (7 years x $25,000), which assumes she will live at least through age 79. However, the full death benefit would be paid out even if she died before making all seven payments. What do you think the death benefit would be for a 72-year-old paying in $175,000 over the next seven years? The answer is $508,000. Keep in mind that the death benefit is guaranteed through age 105 regardless of what happens in the stock market, with interest rates or with the policy's cash value.

Without a doubt, some number crunchers out there are reading this example and saying, "Yeah, but what if she had invested that money instead of buying life insurance? How much would it have grown to by the time of her death?" Naturally, we don't know how long she is going to live, but if she lives to age 90, an equivalent investment would have had to earn 7.3% per year after all fees and taxes. Keep in mind that the death benefit on the life insurance is tax-free and guaranteed. The equivalent annualized rate of return is 5.44% if she lives to age 95, and 4.34% if she lives to 100.

The scenario we never like to talk about is: What if this client gets hit by a bus tomorrow? In that case, the rate of return would be astronomical. We hope that never happens. However, the point we want to make is that as soon as our client made that first premium payment, there was an immediate increase in the value of her estate.

## Life Insurance: Example #2

A married couple, both age 65, have a total net worth of approximately $7 million right now. They do not currently have an estate tax problem based upon where the estate tax exemption stands today ($5 million per person). Therefore, they can pass $10 million (between them) to the next generation free from estate tax. However, they are very frugal, and it is quite likely their estate will eventually surpass the exemption limit. Let's suppose that their estate grows and they end up having $3 million above the exemption limit at the time of the second spouse's death. Approximately a third of the $3 million ($1 million) would go to Uncle Sam to pay estate taxes.

Another aspect of this particular client's case is that approximately half their net worth is tied up in one stock. We were anxious to diversify away some of that risk. However, the stock has a large capital gain. Many people do not want to sell assets that otherwise should be sold just because they do not want to pay the capital gains tax. Life insurance is a perfect solution. Here's how it would work:

We sell $1 million of the stock. Let's assume the cost basis was zero (worst case scenario), so we have a $1 million capital gain and we pay $150,000 in taxes. We take the remaining $850,000 and put it into a "second to die" life insurance policy, which means the death benefit is paid after the second spouse passes away. The guaranteed minimum death benefit is $3.64 million (standard, non-tobacco rate class). The best part is that we can put this policy inside an Irrevocable Life Insurance Trust (ILIT) and the $3.64 million will be outside of their estate and free from any estate taxes.

Life insurance death benefits are almost always income tax free, but they are still considered part of your estate for estate tax purposes. Therefore, if your estate is over the exemption limit ($5 million per person), the death benefit will still be subject to the estate tax. We put this policy inside the ILIT, which removed the policy and death benefit from the couple's estate, thereby possibly saving over $1 million in estate taxes.

## One Final Thought on Life Insurance

If you have a permanent life insurance policy (cash value) that is more than 10 years old, you should have it reviewed by your financial advisor or insurance professional. You may be able to do a tax-free, cost-free exchange for a policy that provides more death benefit for the same premiums. Alternatively, you could reduce your premiums and keep the same death benefit.

## THE STRETCH OR MULTI-GENERATIONAL IRAS

*"We make a living by what we get, but we make a*
*life by what we give."*
— Winston Churchill

You may have heard of the term "Stretch IRA" or "Multi-Generational IRA." It is actually not a category of IRA, such as a Traditional, ROTH, SEP, or SIMPLE; instead, it is more like a financial-planning or wealth-management concept that became available based on some changes in the tax code. In other words, you most likely do not need to do anything to make your current IRA a "Stretch" IRA, but it is good for you to be aware of it for planning purposes. It may change who you name as your beneficiary or the instructions you want to leave that beneficiary.

Years ago, beneficiaries were often required to liquidate the entire inherited IRA as a lump sum or over five years—and pay income tax on the full amount. You can imagine how unhappy people were to lose 30-40% to taxes right off the bat. To make matters worse, some people's IRAs were also part of an estate that was subject to the federal estate tax, making the tax bite much worse. So the IRS changed the tax code, thereby allowing beneficiaries to maintain the tax-deferred status of the account (or tax-free in the case of a ROTH IRA) and simply take Required Minimum Distributions (RMDs) based on their own life expectancies.

The key is to make sure the custodian holding your IRA assets allows beneficiaries to take RMDs over their lifetimes. Most of the big institutional custodians (such as Schwab, TD Ameritrade, Fidelity, and most insurance companies) allow this. However, if your IRA is with a small bank or a non-traditional custodian, it may not be set up to handle lifetime distributions. If that is the case, the beneficiary may be required to take all the money much sooner.

Let's look at an example. Joe's designated beneficiary is his son Bobby. Joe dies in 2008, when he is age 70 and Bobby is age 40. Bobby's life expectancy is an additional 42.7 years (age 82.7) according to the IRS single life expectancy table. That means Bobby is able to withdraw the money he inherited over a period of no more than 42.7 years. If Bobby elects to stretch the distributions over his life expectancy, he must take his first distribution by December 31, 2009, the year-end following the year Joe died.

To determine the minimum amount that must be distributed, Bobby must divide the balance on December 31, 2008 by 42.7. That means his RMD is only 2.35% of the account value. The other 97.65% continues to grow tax-deferred (or tax-free if it's a ROTH). Bobby would also be able to designate a second-generation beneficiary. Let's suppose he designates his daughter Emily. If Bobby were to die in 2029, when his remaining life expectancy would be 22.7 years, Emily could continue distributions for the remaining 22.7 years. She does not get to stretch the balance over her own life expectancy.

Joe could have chosen to designate his granddaughter Emily as his own beneficiary, resulting in a longer distribution period. In such a case, Emily would be the first-generation beneficiary, and her life expectancy, instead of Bobby's, would be used to calculate the RMDs. It may be advantageous to leave IRA money to your youngest beneficiaries since they can leave the money growing tax-deferred for longer and they are likely to be in a lower tax bracket. Look at the example below where Joe left half the money to his son Bobby and half to his granddaughter Emily[1]:

| Joe dies, leaving his $256,000 IRA to be split equally between his son, age 40, and granddaughter, age 12 | | | |
|---|---|---|---|
| | Inherited amount | If paying lump sum tax @ 35% | If Stretch IRA, taking RMD over life expectancy, assume 7% annual investment return |
| Bobby, age 40 | $128,000 | $83,200 | $821,000 |
| Emily, age 12 | $128,000 | $83,200 | $3,405,647 |

## Tax Deferral

The primary benefit of the stretch provision is that it allows the beneficiaries to defer paying taxes on the account balance and to continue enjoying tax-deferred and/or tax-free growth as long as possible. Without the stretch provision, beneficiaries may be required to distribute the full account balance in a period much shorter than the beneficiary's life expectancy. A shorter distribution period may cause them to be in a higher tax bracket.

## Flexibility

Some custodians allow you to use a "restricted" beneficiary designation, which forces the beneficiary to take the money over his or her lifetime or some set number of years. However, the stretch option is generally not a binding provision, which means the beneficiary may choose to withdraw more than the minimum any time he or she needs or wants it.

---

1   Note: This example is hypothetical and does not represent any specific investment. Actual results will vary. Past performance does not guarantee future results.

## Benefits for Spouses

A spousal beneficiary is allowed to treat the inherited IRA as his or her own, which is usually preferable. So you should only think of the stretch concept when leaving your IRA to the next generation or at least someone other than your spouse.

## FUNDING COLLEGE EDUCATION FOR LOVED ONES

*"Generosity lies less in giving much than in giving at the right moment."*
— Jean De La Brutere

Many of our clients want to make sure their grandkids have money to go to college. An education is arguably one of the greatest gifts you can give to anyone. The cost of higher education today is staggering, and there seems to be no end in sight for tuition increases, which have averaged about 8% per year.[2] An 8% college inflation rate means that the cost of college doubles every nine years. Most  college students are financing their way through college with the help of the great American invention we call "Credit."

The average college graduate in 2010 graduated with $25,250 in student loan debt. Of course, some graduates do not have any student loans, which means others have significantly more than the average. That much debt is a tough way to start your career. In the first quarter

---

2   Source: www.finaid.org/savings/tuition-inflation

of 2011, total outstanding student loan debt nationwide surpassed total credit card debt for the first time! Additionally, student loan debt cannot be discharged by declaring personal bankruptcy. You must pay it all back! Congress recognized the problem (so it says) and has provided tax incentives for people to save for college, including 529 plans.

The section 529 plan is now the preferred and most recommended college savings plan. 529 plans have always had significant tax benefits. However, concern arose because many of those benefits were scheduled to expire after 2010. The Pension Protection Act of 2006 made many section 529 plan provisions permanent. Thus, you should definitely consider a 529 plan if you are looking for a way to fund your children or grandchildren's college education. Almost any financial advisor can set these accounts up for you. Here is a quick overview of how they work:

### The basic two 529 plans

Savings Plans and Prepaid Tuition plans are both forms of section 529 plans. Many states offer Prepaid Tuition plans that allow you to pay a fixed amount to a specific state institution now for a guarantee that your child's tuition will be covered at that state institution when he or she attends it in the future. This plan may be a good deal. If tuition continues to increase at 8% a year, it is like having an investment with a guaranteed 8% return as long as your student ends up going to that institution.

College savings plans are more commonly used because they are more flexible. The savings plans enable you to invest money to be used for the beneficiary's future higher education expenses. Your money is typically invested in mutual funds offered by the plan, with no guarantee as to how much will be available when the beneficiary enters college. The savings plans allow you to use the account value at any Eligible Educational Institution, which includes most community colleges, public and private colleges and universities, and vocational schools.

## The tax benefits of section 529 plans are significant.

Earnings in the plan are withdrawn tax free as long as they are used to pay for qualified higher education expenses, which include tuition, books, and certain other fees and expenses such as computer technology or Internet access.

## Significant sums can be saved through section 529 plans.

Individuals can take advantage of the annual gift tax exclusion by contributing up to $13,000 ($26,000 for married couples) per beneficiary, per year. A special rule applicable only to 529 plans allows an individual to accelerate up to five years' worth of annual exclusions by contributing up to $65,000 ($130,000 for married couples) in one calendar year. While no gift taxes are payable, the donor can only take advantage of this special rule by making an election on a federal gift tax return, IRS Form 709. If you take advantage of this rule, additional contributions or gifts to the beneficiary may exceed the annual gift exclusion. Grandparents can set up accounts for grandchildren, transferring large sums from their estates (potentially reducing future estate taxes) while providing for their grandchildren's education.

**Section 529 plans are treated favorably for financial aid purposes.**

Section 529 plans are no longer considered the child's asset. If the plan is set up by the parent, only up to 5.6 % of the value will be counted toward the expected family contribution. Withdrawals from the plans are also no longer considered income for financial aid purposes. Prior to July 2006, withdrawals reduced financial aid on a dollar-for-dollar basis.

**Funds aren't lost if the beneficiary does not go to college.**

A significant advantage of section 529 plans is that you remain the account owner. Thus, you can change the beneficiary or even take the money back, if permitted by the plan. If you take the money back, you will owe ordinary income taxes on earnings and a 10% federal tax penalty. However, the money can be withdrawn without penalty if the beneficiary dies or becomes disabled.

**Many plans are now available.**

There are over 80 different 529 plans available since many states offer more than one plan. You can invest in any state's plan, no matter which state you live in. Some states offer state income tax benefits to residents who contribute to their state's plan. Each plan has different investment options and fees, so talk to your financial advisor before making a choice. Alternatively, you can research it yourself on dozens of websites such as **www.savingforcollege.com.**

## "OPEN AFTER I'M GONE": A "WHAT IF" LETTER AND FINANCIAL INVENTORY

We strongly believe that one of the most underutilized tools in legacy planning is a simple "what if" letter. In other words, what if you don't make it home from the grocery store? What would you like to convey to your loved ones? Your Will or your Trust simply states who gets what. It most likely does not contain a narrative of instructions,

memories, or your wishes for your beneficiaries. The vast majority of people never write a "what if" letter because they don't really want to consider their own mortality or because they don't know where to start. Below are some pointers and sample letters that hopefully will get you started on your own letter.

**There should be two separate components to the letter:**

1. <u>Financial Inventory & Instructions</u>: Typically when someone dies, the beneficiaries search the house and file cabinets trying to figure out what assets you have. Some accounts and valuables are listed in your will or revocable living trust, but many are not. In addition, the typical estate planning documents do not have contact information for your professional advisors, user names and passwords for your accounts, or notes and instructions. You ought to specify the location and approximate value of your important possessions. Your major accounts may have named beneficiaries, but what about sentimental pieces like

jewelry, art, or vehicles. Specify exactly which sentimental items go to whom. Your Financial Inventory will make things much easier for your surviving spouse and/or your other beneficiaries. However, it will also prove to be a valuable tool for you by forcing you to organize your financial life.[3]

2. <u>A Heartfelt Letter</u>: This letter is your last chance to share your memories, thoughts, values, and wishes with your heirs. Give the letter a personal touch by addressing each of your heirs and beneficiaries personally. Tell them any last wishes you may have or any hopes you have for their future.

Keep a copy of the letter at home with your estate planning documents and one with your attorney. Storing it in a safety deposit box might make it difficult for your beneficiaries to access. Update the letter frequently to make sure it says what you really want to say.

Here are a couple of sample "what if" letters to give you some ideas:

**Sample "What If" Letter to My Children**

Dear Katie & Dana,

If you are reading this letter, I have probably passed away. Please do not be sad. I want you to know that I led a full and fulfilling life. Raising the two of you was my greatest joy, and ultimately, my family is my greatest accomplishment. I am so proud of each one of you. We have been very fortunate, and I am so happy that I was able to leave some money behind for each of you and for my precious grandchildren (Tyler, Brooke,

---

3   See Sample Financial Inventory in Appendix B.

Michael, and Isabelle). My trust specifies who gets what. In a nutshell, I wanted to split up my assets in such a way that you each get 40% of my estate and the other 20% gets split equally between my grandkids.

Splitting up the money is relatively easy when it comes to real estate or investment accounts. It was a bit more difficult to figure out who should get which piece of jewelry, art, furniture, my car, etc. There is a list of specific bequests with my living trust that indicates who gets what. I tried to guess who would want each item. I need you to know that it was not my intention to favor any one of you, and I tried to make the bequests as even as possible. The only thing I ask is please do not fight over any of this. I would feel terrible to think that my bequests led to any hard feelings. Feel free to trade things amongst yourselves or sell anything you do not want to keep. My feelings will not be hurt if you do not want to lug my collection of first edition books around for the rest of your lives.

More important than what I am leaving each of you financially are my final thoughts and wishes. Here are a few things that I have always believed and I hope you will also adopt:

1. Always Put Family First: There will be plenty of times when you have to choose between career (or other demands) and family. I know that choosing family is not always easy and frequently requires sacrifice. I just want you to know that I treasure every memory I have of you guys as kids and adults. The money and accomplishments mean very little in comparison to the memories of you when you were young. I hope you will always choose family. I am not going to tell

you what to do with the money I left behind, but I hope each of you will use it to make your life more enjoyable and less stressful. It makes me happy to think of you using your inheritance to take more family vacations, to help your kids through college, and to pursue hobbies and interests that you find fulfilling.

Please always support each other. If you disagree about something, let it go and forgive each other. Any time or experiences that you miss with each other or with your kids will be irreplaceable.

2. Never Sacrifice Your Integrity: In this world, there are so many chances to make a quick buck, lie to your spouse, walk away from your debts, etc. It seems like these days nothing is taboo anymore. Our society accepts a lower moral standard than I grew up with. I hope you will always act honorably. Don't take the easy way out. Throughout my life, I found that when faced with two roads, the more difficult one was usually the right one to take.

3. Always Give Back: We are all so fortunate. Many people have never had the opportunities that you kids have had. Please help those who need help. Find a cause that means something to you and get involved. Also, please instill this virtue of giving in your children. It makes the world a better place and I have found that the donor usually gets more out of it than the recipient.

Now a few thoughts for each of you individually:

Katie: I still remember the day you were born at Summerlin Hospital in Las Vegas. You seemed to be perfect from the moment you entered the world. Eventually, I found out that you weren't perfect, like the time you snuck out of the house in high school or the time you wrecked my new car in college. Anyway, I couldn't have loved you more. If someone would ask me to describe you in a sentence, I would say that you are the most genuine, generous, sensitive, and beautiful person I have ever known. I used to worry that you were too sensitive and your feelings would get hurt too easily. I thought this tough world might chew you up and spit you out. To my great joy, not only did that not happen, but you have maintained your honest, open, generous nature. In other words, you did not let the world change you. Bravo! You are a rare breed and I am proud of you.

Dana: There is no one who has given me more laughs in my lifetime than you. What a wonderful gift. You have been funny and silly from the time you were a toddler. I always admired that quality because I felt that perhaps I took life too seriously, especially when I was younger. You may not realize it, but you helped me see life in a more balanced perspective. You also were known for your temper. Your mom and I used to joke that you had two speeds, really happy or really pissed off. I remember one time when you were a little kid and your Aunt Susan was at the house. You were in a bad mood and I commented that you were not easy. Your Aunt Susan said it perfectly. She said, "Dana marches to her own drummer. She is only difficult if you expect her to follow the path of everyone else." You have always done things your way. Sometimes that has turned out better than others, but I want you to know that I admire you. I think a great many people wish they were more like you. You are a leader and you are unique and precious. Most importantly, you are a great sister and a great mom.

Love Always, Dad

## Sample "What If" Letter to My Wife

Dear Mary,

If you are reading this letter, I have probably passed away. I can't believe you outlasted me! Thank you for being my partner in life for the last 60+ years. My mother told me when I was young that I needed to marry a strong woman…and I did. I am sure that living without me will be a bit of an adjustment, but I hope you will adjust quickly and get on with life. I hope you live many more years, and that your next chapter will be filled with new people, new places, and more quality time with our kids and grandkids. I may not have been the easiest person to live with, so thanks for putting up with me. You were a good wife and a good mother.

I have organized our financial life so you can pick up right where I left off…paying bills! All joking aside, you will find our financial inventory statement inside our trust binder with account numbers, user names and passwords, phone numbers, and notes. Before you do anything, please meet with our financial advisor (Jeremy Kisner) and our attorney (Richard Chatwin). If you ever get conflicting financial advice, follow whatever Mr. Kisner says. As you know, I have gotten to know him very well over the years and I trust him implicitly.

It may be hard to think about this right now, but maybe one day you will remarry. I want you to know that you have my blessings. My only request is that you keep your money separate and make sure our kids inherit what's left after you join me in heaven. I'll be waiting for you there…but don't rush.

Your Loving Husband,

P.S. Feel free to sell my collection of first edition books. Just don't throw them out or sell them at a garage sale. It may be hard to believe, but people will pay a lot of money for those things.

**CHAPTER 7**

# MYTHS, MISCONCEPTIONS, AND "STUPID" IDEAS

---

*"Faced with a choice between changing one's mind and proving there is no need to do so, almost everyone gets busy on the proof."*
— John Kenneth Galbraith

### Made–Up Minds

Once a person has made up his or her mind, it's hard to get the person to change it, no matter how logical the arguments may be. The following is a rather extreme example, but it shows that many people have a tendency to realign any new evidence or information to match their preconceived notions. Chris Mooney remarked upon this tendency in an article entitled "The Science of Why We Don't Believe Science"[1]:

> **"A MAN WITH A CONVICTION** is a hard man to change. Tell him you disagree and he turns away. Show him facts or figures and he questions your sources. Appeal to logic and

---

1   Mooney, Chris. "The Science of Why We Don't Believe Science." *Mother Jones Magazine.* (March 2011). http://motherjones.com/politics/2011/03/denial-science-chris-mooney. Accessed September 23, 2011.

he fails to see your point." So wrote the celebrated Stanford University psychologist Leon Festinger....

Festinger and several of his colleagues had infiltrated the Seekers, a small Chicago-area cult whose members thought they were communicating with aliens....the aliens had given the precise date of an Earth-rending cataclysm: December 21, 1954.... Festinger and his team were with the cult when the prophecy failed....It was the moment Festinger had been waiting for: How would people so emotionally invested in a belief system react, now that it had been soundly refuted?

At first, the group struggled for an explanation. But then rationalization set in. A new message arrived, announcing that they'd all been spared at the last minute....

In the annals of denial, it doesn't get much more extreme than the Seekers....And since Festinger's day, an array of new discoveries in psychology and neuroscience has further demonstrated how our preexisting beliefs, far more than any new facts, can skew our thoughts and even color what we consider our most dispassionate and logical conclusions. This tendency toward so-called "motivated reasoning" helps explain why we find groups so polarized over matters where the evidence is so unequivocal: vaccines, "death panels," the birthplace and religion of the president, and much else. It would seem that expecting people to be convinced by the facts flies in the face of, you know, the facts.

The theory of motivated reasoning builds on a key insight of modern neuroscience: Reasoning is actually suffused with emotion (or what researchers often call "affect"). Not only are the two inseparable, but our positive or negative feelings about people, things, and ideas arise much more rapidly than our conscious thoughts, in a matter of milliseconds—fast enough to detect with an EEG device, but long before we're aware of it. That shouldn't be surprising: Evolution required us to react very quickly to stimuli in our environment. It's a "basic human survival skill," explains political scientist Arthur Lupia of the University of Michigan. We push threatening information away; we pull friendly information close....

In other words, when we think we're reasoning, we may instead be rationalizing.

So what's the upshot of all this? We all wear blinders sometimes and cling stubbornly to our pre-existing beliefs. After all, it is not human nature to give up a belief system that was built up over a lifetime because of some new snippet of information. In fact, people who are willing to change their views are sometimes labeled as "flip-floppers." With that as a backdrop, we will now give you some of the myths, misconceptions, and stupid ideas we see in our role as investment advisors and financial planners.

## MYTH #1: GETTING INVESTMENT IDEAS FROM THE MEDIA

*"I'm tired of hearing about money, money, money, money. I just want to play the game, drink Pepsi, and wear Reebok."*
— Shaquille O'Neal

There is no doubt that people are influenced by what they see, read, and hear. The media wants to keep your attention so it can sell advertising and subscriptions. You constantly see compelling headlines like: "Beat the Market!", "The 10 Best Stocks Right Now!", "Get Rich

Trading!" and "The New Five-Star Fund Rankings!" TV personalities fuel the fire even further, with some of them ranting and raving. We call this **"financial pornography"** because it is very compelling to watch but should only be considered for its entertainment value. Nevertheless, this financial pornography sways the decisions of even seemingly rational investors. Unfortunately, designing an investment plan based on what you see in the media usually turns out to be disastrous.

On any given day, you can turn on the TV and get an in-depth analysis explaining why the market is going to move in a certain direction. Then, surprisingly, the market does the exact opposite of what was predicted and new reasoning is given for that. An industry joke: "What's the definition of an economist? An expert who will know tomorrow why the things he predicted yesterday didn't happen today." The truth is that short-term fluctuations are nearly random and cannot be predicted with any accuracy or consistency.

Sadly, investors faced with a high degree of uncertainty will turn to any plausible explanation and can be influenced by very flawed reasoning, especially if it is delivered with conviction. Studies show that even useless information can influence decisions. Consider this example from *The Little Book of Behavioral Investing* by James Montier. Montier tells how psychologists set up a clever experiment in which they waited for a line to form at a photocopier and had someone try to cut in line. First they tried the experiment where the person asks to cut in line but does not give any reason. The second time the person gave a reason, saying, "Excuse me, I have five pages to copy. May I use the Xerox machine, because I'm in a rush?" Surprisingly 60 percent of people allowed the person without any reason to cut in line, and 90% of people allowed the one whose reason was "I'm in a rush" to cut. The study also noted that whenever people gave a reason using the word "because" 90% of people said, "Yes," regardless of the reason.

One conclusion of this study was that people are persuaded by reasons regardless of how ridiculous or meaningless they may be. In life, it is good to be an optimist, but as investors, it sometimes pays to be a bit more skeptical. We should start asking ourselves, "Why shouldn't I believe this?" instead of "Can I believe this?"

**Our Advice When Considering a Recommendation:**

1. Consider the source of your financial advice.

2. Don't be afraid to question the reasons given for a recommendation.

## MYTH #2: INSURANCE IS A RIP-OFF

It is surprising how many people we meet are anti-insurance. I always ask them why? The answers usually fall into two categories:

1. <u>I don't need insurance</u>. This belief is true in some cases especially for wealthy clients who can afford to self-insure. However, it is frequently a symptom of many of the behavioral biases we have discussed in the book (denial, better than average effect, recency bias).

2. <u>Insurance is a rip-off</u>. This belief is never based on any type of analysis. Some people just look at insurance as a gamble and hate the idea that the statistics are on the insurance company's side. In other words, if everything works out as expected, this policy will be profitable for the insurance company, which must mean it was a waste of money for me.

The typical response to these objections from insurance agents and financial advisors is to try to prove the value (or need) using statistics and probability. We are not going to do that (although we could) because these decisions are not about the math. They are about the human consequences of your decisions. Let us share a story from our practice:

Approximately six years ago, a really nice couple came to meet with us after attending one of our seminars. The couple had recently retired and had a whole host of questions and issues. One question was whether they should keep a $150,000 life insurance policy that they had on the wife. The premium was due and they figured they didn't need the insurance anymore. However, this was *not* a "no-brainer" decision.

- They had enough retirement income but not a surplus.

- Their house was paid for and their kids were grown and self-sufficient.

- It was term insurance and only five years were left on the term.

- The wife seemed perfectly healthy; hence, the likely scenario was that she was going to outlive the term (the insurance would end up lapsing anyway).

- Lastly, their inclination was to let the policy lapse.

Nevertheless, we reviewed the policy in context of their overall financial situation and advised them to pay the premium and keep the policy. The good news is they followed our advice. The bad news is, three months later, she was diagnosed with liver cancer and died within six months of our original meeting.

I remember visiting her at her home shortly before her death. She was still very alert despite her poor physical condition. She wanted to tell me two things. She asked me to look out for her husband after she was gone, and she thanked me for telling her to keep her life insurance. The interesting epilogue to this story is that the $150,000 death benefit they didn't think they needed was needed. Six years later, it has been completely spent by the husband due to unforeseen expenses. Life can be unpredictable.

You probably think we are pro-insurance. We are not, and we certainly do not believe in over-insuring. However, insurance definitely has its place. The reason we are financial planners is to enable you to live an extraordinary life and a life you love. Why would you risk that because you are afraid that the insurance company might make a profit on you? In fact, we feel the opposite. You should hope you are a very profitable client for the insurance company because that will mean you never died prematurely, became disabled, got in a car accident, went to a nursing home, and your house never burned down. You should never regret paying premiums on those policies because knowing that your family and your life savings are protected should enable you to sleep at night with the comfort that you have responsibly planned for your loved ones. If, on the other hand, one of those unfortunate events does occur, at least the emotional toll on you and/or your family will not be compounded by financial stress and uncertainty.

Buying insurance is not a gamble. Not buying it is.

**Our Advice When Buying Insurance:**

1. Transfer the risks that could wipe you out (death, disability, long-term care).

2. Work with an independent agent who can shop many carriers for the best price.

3. Re-evaluate every few years. New cutting edge products can serve dual purposes (e.g. life insurance where the death benefit can be accessed while you're still alive to pay for long-term care).

## MYTH #3: THE MARKET AVERAGES 10% PER YEAR

Most financial advisors and investors figure that the stock market returns an average of 10% per year. Some years will be better and some worse, but 10% seems to be the average number most people use. This rate of return may be true if you look at very long periods of time:

- From 1900 through 2010, the average annualized return for the DJIA (Dow Jones Industrial Average) was approximately 9.4%, including 4.8% in price appreciation, plus approx 4.7% in dividends. (Some numbers won't add up due to rounding.) In 2010, the average dividend yield on the DJIA was only about 2.5%, so these days, investors are relying more on price appreciation if they are expecting similar returns.

- Since 1929 (End-of-year 1928—i.e., before the crash) thru 2010, the return was 8.8% (4.6%, plus 4.3%).

- Since end-of-year 1932 (i.e., after the crash): 11.2% (7.0%, plus 4.2%).

Unfortunately, the average retirement is not 80 years; it is only 20. Let's consider that timeframe. If you invest $100,000 for 20 years and do not take any withdrawals, how much will you have? The answer is: You don't know. If you assume a 10% rate of return, you are expecting your $100,000 to grow to $672,750. However, the range of results, if you look at every 20-year period over the past 100 years, is your $100,000 could have averaged 2.5% and turned into approximately $163,000 (1928-1947), or it could have averaged approximately 18% and turned into over $2.7 million (1979-1998).

The stock market has significant variations and volatility from year to year, but if you take a step back, you will see long-term patterns. We have distinct upward trends (bull markets) and distinct downward or sideways trends (bear markets). If you look at the last eight decades, only three had average annualized returns in excess of 10% (the '50s, '80s, and '90s). Those three decades were very profitable and crushed the 10% long-term number. However, if you were expecting 10% per year, the other five decades would have underperformed your expectations (sometimes significantly). Also, keep in mind that all of these numbers exclude the impact of taxes, inflation, fees, or transaction costs.

Before you get too down on stocks, keep in mind that over the long-term, they have significantly outperformed every other major investable asset class.

What is the point? You must be careful when relying on averages. People retiring today spent most of their adult life in the 25-year period from 1982-2007. This timeframe included the largest bull market in history and two of the best decades ever in the stock market. This period has colored people's expectations for the future and led them to believe that returns of 5-9% are too low.

**Our Advice on Expected Market Returns:**

1. Use conservative assumptions regarding future returns.

2. Don't make too big of a bet on one asset class. You should probably have stocks in your portfolio, but also include more alternative asset classes (see Appendix A) to produce smoother and more predictable returns.

3. Diversify—not just by type of investment, but by strategy. For example, have things in your investment portfolio that do well in times of high inflations (e.g. commodities) and also low inflation (bonds).

## MYTH #4: I'LL JUST LIVE OFF OF THE INTEREST AND NEVER TOUCH THE PRINCIPAL

This myth is one of the most widely held "stupid ideas." Don't be insulted if this was your plan and now we are throwing cold water on it. Living off the interest sounds good to most people, and many people cling to it even in the face of irrefutable data that it is probably the worst investment strategy you can have. I should temper that last statement by saying it is the worst investment strategy you can have *if* your objective is to grow your money or to provide inflation-adjusted income you won't outlive. The plan only to spend your interest and never touch your principal completely ignores inflation and the unpredictability of interest rates.

A couple of years back, a seminar attendee came up to us after our presentation and said he wanted to book our first available appointment and was going to transfer all of his money to us to manage. When he came into our office, we found out that all of his money was in municipal and treasury bonds and had been for the previous 25 years. He wanted us to buy him new bonds as the ones he owned matured. This situation could have been a case study in "what not to do" and we did not take him on as a client. Let's take a closer look at why what he was asking us to do was a bad idea:

Sam (not his real name) had been the CEO of a major corporation. At one time, he had 2,000 people working for him. He retired in 1984 with $2 million. That is still a lot of money today, but it was a heck of a lot more money back in 1984. Sam put all his money into bonds and planned to live off the interest. His average interest rate when he set up this bond portfolio was approximately 9% so his income was $180,000 per year ($2 million x 9%). He was able to live pretty comfortably in 1984 on that level of income. Keep in mind that this is a person who was used to flying first class, traveling the world, and buying a new car every couple of years. Fast forward 25 years to 2009—Inflation over his 25-year retirement period had totaled 107% (according to the CPI), so he would have needed $372,000 to have the same buying power he did when he retired. Unfortunately, interest rates had come down substantially to an average of 4.5% so his income had dropped to $90,000 and he was now supporting himself partly from the principal. Since we met Sam, interest rates have continued to drop. We heard through an estate planning attorney we know that Sam passed away last year at the age of 85, but his healthy wife, who is only 70 years old, could certainly live another 20-25 years and run out of money.

Any study of income distribution strategies will show that putting all of your money in safe money assets (CDs, bonds) is the surest way to go broke in retirement. A better approach is a diversified investment plan that includes "growth" assets like stocks, real estate, and commodities. You will have to do some systematic liquidations and rebalancing in order to supply the necessary income since this diversified portfolio will likely "yield" less in terms of dividends and interest than the all-bond portfolio. However, the growth assets should more than replace the withdrawals. These higher growth assets are what provide the ability to increase income to keep pace with inflation (assuming a safe withdrawal rate, which varies depending on your age and the composition of the portfolio).

The best approach takes the diversified portfolio one step further by segmenting the portfolio into short-term and long-term assets. The short-term money is invested in safe liquid assets used to provide income for the next few years. This money is spent down (principal and interest). The purpose of the short-term money that gets spent down is to give the longer-term growth assets time to grow. This strategy is frequently called a "buckets of money" approach. The strategy we use is called Income Harvesting (see the "Investing for Income" section of this book). Periodically, you have to "Harvest" some of the growth assets and replenish the short-term income bucket. We realize this strategy sounds a bit complex. We also realize that spending down principal in one portion of your portfolio and not touching another portion sounds counter-intuitive. I wish it were simpler. The bottom line is that this topic has been researched extensively and the approach described above is what works.

### Our Advice on Planning For Lifetime Income:

Work with a Financial Advisor who understands how to plan properly for income distribution.

## MYTH #5: THE RULE OF 100

We have always found this rule to be comically simplistic. The "rule," as it is described in finance books and on websites, is that you should subtract your age from 100 and the result will be the maximum you should have in stocks. For example, if you are 70, then you should have no more than 30% of your money in stocks. Nice story if you are trying to get someone to sell his stocks and put the money in a fixed annuity. However, it raises a few questions:

- Is the amount you should have in stocks limited to stocks, or is it any type of variable investment? Doesn't the amount you should have in stocks (or any investment for that matter) depend on your objectives, your health, your risk tolerance, your income needs?

- Does it matter what type of stocks you are investing in, or are small biotech stocks the same as owning utility stocks?

- Don't valuations matter? If bonds are trading at all time highs (interest rates are at all time lows) shouldn't that override a simplistic rule that says put 70% in fixed assets?

**Our Advice in Choosing What Percentage to Invest in Stocks:**

Run in the other direction if an investment advisor uses the Rule of 100 to justify his or her recommendations. You should be looking for an investment advisor who tailors his or her advice to you based on your specific goals, risk tolerance, and income needs. Good financial planning is not cookie cutter. If it were this simple, the profession of financial planning would be on the endangered species list.

## MYTH #6: I'M GOING TO MAKE A FORTUNE NOW THAT I KNOW HOW TO READ THESE CHARTS

> *"If past history was all there was to the game, the richest people would be librarians."*
> — Warren Buffet

Occasionally, we run into investors who practice the fine art of "Technical Analysis." In the '90s, they were called day traders. Technical analysis is a method of analyzing an investment by using recent trading volume and price movement to identify patterns and thereby predict the next price movement. People who rely on technical analysis seem intent on proving the saying "A little knowledge is a dangerous thing." They typically have not been doing this for long because it typically doesn't take too long before they lose all or most of their money. However, they do sound smart.

Individuals who use technical analysis typically do not hire financial advisors. They are what we call do-it-yourself-ers. They generally speculate on short-term trades in commodities, options, or individual stocks. Technical analysis used to work a lot better, but it really hasn't worked too well for the past 10 years. Most serious money managers use technical analysis only to confirm their other research. For example, in our firm, we start with quantitative analysis, which is helpful in narrowing down a list of potential investments by looking at dozens of financial ratios. Once we narrow down the list using quantitative analysis, we do fundamental analysis, which includes the study of the company's industry, products, competition, trends, management, etc. This process enables us to narrow down the list further, and hopefully, to identify a company in which we would like to invest. Then technical analysis is the last step, which is used simply to see whether our research is confirmed by the flow of money from institutional buyers into the investment.

Unfortunately, most individual investors do not have the tools, resources, knowledge, or patience to do that much research. Therefore, they just do part of the research. Technical analysis seems really cool. Many retail investors can easily get dazzled by someone who talks over their head ("This guy is smart."). They assume that because someone is spouting off about "Fibinaci Retracement Levels," he must know what he is doing. I assure you that is frequently not the case.

As mentioned earlier in the book, short-term trading and charting works until it doesn't, and then you may be broke. "Stop Loss" orders are great until your stock "gaps" down 50% overnight. When a stock gaps down, it may go from $100 a share to $50 with no trades in between. In other words, the stock could close at $100, but if bad news comes out after the market is closed, when it re-opens the stock could be at $50. This is a problem if you had a stop loss at $95 because you would be selling at $50. Another problem would be if you sell your entire position in Procter and Gamble for $40 per share before it closes that same day at $61, like we watched happen to many people on May 6, 2010 during the "flash crash."

Don't get us wrong; you can get lucky and sometimes be lucky for quite awhile. Please trust us though when we say that the odds are you will lose and lose big when trying to make money on short-term trading. It's like our clients in Las Vegas always say, "This town wasn't built on winners." At least in Vegas, they give you free drinks while you are losing your money. We have seen the biggest and the brightest with the most sophisticated algorithms and fastest computers wiped out by unforeseeable events. The decks are stacked against you, so proceed at your own peril. Our experience in technical analysis has shown that it is a great tool to help establish entry and exit points in an investment, but only after days of other research have been done. To think that you can manage your retirement-based chart patterns, software tools, and signals you read or purchase is foolish. It would make our lives much easier if we could just follow a 50 or 200-day moving average to decide whether to buy or respond to our favorite sell signal and know then to sell everything. It just doesn't work that easily!

## The Death Cross

Some of you reading this book may remember in 2010 when the financial media was cautioning about the Death Cross forming in the markets? The pundits were telling you to run for the exits because the S&P was going to retest the 2009 lows. That's because the 50-day moving average had just crossed the 200-day moving average, a very ominous sign. It happened around July 12, 2010 when the S&P 500 was at 1022. Twelve months later (July of 2011), the S&P 500 was at 1339, a devastating loss....I mean gain of 31%! That wasn't supposed to happen. Yet headline after headline frightened people to the sidelines. We had 80-year-old clients asking whether we thought we should sell their stock because of the Death Cross. That's how crazy this stuff is. The human mind so desperately wants to believe that you can reduce complex, random, and sometimes irrational markets into a pattern recognition system that follows simple moving averages. Buy on green, sell on red. People spend hundreds of millions of dollars each year attending seminars and buying software and books that promise the ability to predict the market's next move. Every day, guys on the radio are saying, "You have to know how to read the charts! I can teach you how to read the charts! Just follow our signals...blah, blah, blah."

Let's ask ourselves a few questions: Don't we have supercomputers these days that could be programmed to read these charts? Wouldn't every major mutual fund have teams of people who know how to read charts? Isn't 65% of the trading on the New York Stock Exchange done by high frequency traders using supercomputers to take advantage of split-second one penny price discrepancies between market makers? Do you really think you can act on information you got from looking at a chart before the millions of people who work on Wall Street? This "read the charts" advice just doesn't pass the common sense test.

**Our Advice on Charting and Technical Analysis:**

1. Resist the temptation to make short-term speculative trades regardless of how compelling the story sounds.

2. Lengthen your holding periods, invest in a more diverse set of asset classes, buy world class independent research, and implement a risk discipline. If you are not comfortable doing this, hire someone who can help you, but don't waste your time or money on technical analysis tools whose value is quite limited.

## MYTH #7: PASSIVE VS. ACTIVE INVESTING

A large contingent of smart people think you cannot beat the market by picking individual stocks or industries. Furthermore, the costs involved with mutual funds or other actively managed investment vehicles (i.e. mutual funds or individual stocks) outweigh any potential advantage. In other words, you should just buy and hold an index fund (ETF) that represents a segment of the market (e.g. S&P 500 for large cap domestic stocks) and mirrors its performance. This advice is not the worst we have ever heard, but a few insights should be added.

First, passive investing works well in a rising market. It was a great strategy from 1982-2000. But it has not worked so well from 2000-2011 because the market has been flat. Admittedly, some active money managers have likely done worse. However, the real problem with passive investing (buy and hold) is that it really limits your risk-management abilities. An active money manager can buy more of what is on sale and reduce exposure to asset classes that are overvalued.

One frequently quoted statistic by those in favor of passive investing is that 70% of mutual funds underperform their benchmark. These people say, "Why not just buy an index fund whose performance will mirror the index and outperform 70% of the mutual funds?" The 70% figure is roughly true for large cap domestic stock funds. Large U.S. companies may have 30 analysts covering every move a company makes and all money managers are working off the same information. However, that's not the case for less transparent asset classes (e.g. small cap emerging markets).

## Our Advice Regarding Passive vs. Active Investing

We believe that passive or indexed strategies make more sense in efficient markets where outperformance is less likely; therefore, you might want to focus on cost control. The corollary is that in inefficient areas like emerging markets, we feel it may be well worth the money paid for a good manager (i.e. mutual fund). Several good active mutual fund managers have consistently beaten their benchmarks over the past decade in these inefficient asset classes. The biggest thing we want to stress here is that while fees are important, they are not everything. A passive indexing strategy over the past decade was cheap, but you likely lost money. Paying low fees to lose money is not very satisfying. We would rather pay 1-2% for an actively managed fund that we believe will deliver significantly better results. Sometimes the old adage "you get what you pay for" rings true.

# CHAPTER 8

# WORKING WITH
# A FINANCIAL ADVISOR

*"Wall Street is the only place that people ride to in a Rolls Royce to get advice from those who take the subway."*
— *Warren Buffett*

Few things will affect you and your family more over the coming decades than the financial decisions you are making today. We have seen countless people amass small fortunes during their lifetimes only to squander them through bad financial decisions. We are all familiar with the celebrities who have lost it all (see sidebar on next page). What is not reported in the press is how many middle class millionaires also lose it all. And an even larger group do not lose it all but could have left a legacy for generations if they had made better financial decisions.

Many people go to seminars looking to find an investment for a particular chunk of money. What they should be looking for is a trusted advisor they can stick with for the rest of their lives. A good advisor can be worth his or her weight in gold. The relationship should provide comfort and confidence. Think of this trusted advisor as a coach who helps you to focus on what's important at just the right time and can provide insight and perspective.

Unfortunately, not all financial advisors are created equal. There is such a thing as bad financial advice, just like there is bad medical advice, bad legal advice, etc. Many people reading this book may have been victims of bad financial advice. That's okay. Don't get discouraged. On the next few pages, we are going to help you become an "educated consumer of financial services" so you can find a financial advisor who is right for you.

## Don't Hire a "Yes Man" (or Woman)

The first thing to point out is that a good advisor is not always going to agree with you. Remember, you are not looking for a "yes" man (or woman). It is a fact that people consistently underestimate their probability of getting sick, losing a job, becoming disabled, dying prematurely, running out of money and almost everything else that is unpleasant. It is your financial advisor's job to help you prepare for all these things that you don't think will ever happen.

One of the biggest mistakes financial advisors make is they are afraid to disagree with you. They want to tell you whatever you want to hear: "Of course, Mr. Client, you have worked hard and you deserve to retire. I would be happy to roll over this retirement account for you." That may have been what you wanted to hear and what the financial advisor wants to say. However, the right answer may have been, "I am sorry to tell you this, but you don't have enough money to retire unless you are prepared to cut your living expenses by $10,000 a year." That is a tougher message to deliver. Many advisors will go along with the client's worst ideas and most self-destructive choices, especially if they make the advisor money. This practice has cost our industry its trust, which is currently at an all time low. In a recent study[1], 27% of those surveyed said they did not trust their primary financial advisor. It is time for financial advisors to stop being enablers and to realize their role is to protect their clients, not sell them products.

It would be nice if the average client appreciated the honesty, but frequently, they just go to the next guy who tells them what they want to hear or promises juicier returns. People typically seek out others who already agree with their pre-existing beliefs. We are limited by our own **confirmation bias**, in which we only see what confirms our already held beliefs and ignore the rest. Just think about the news channel you watch, the publications you read, the talk radio you listen to. For example, who do you think listens to conservative talk radio? It's not liberals or even people in the middle of the political spectrum. It's people who already have distinct conservative beliefs. And that's true for any media source or "talking head." Are you seeking out contradictory opinions in hopes of understanding a different point of view? Most people are not. So, here is a bit of advice; although it

1 Source: Survey: Sullivan Insights on Affluent Investors for Financial Marketers, 2009.

goes against human nature—if your advisor disagrees with you, take the time (and patience) to understand why. Don't just ignore the advice.

## HOW YOUR ADVISOR GETS PAID

We had one client who managed sales forces for a living. He told us that he could do a lot of things wrong and still be successful. He just had to get three things right with his sales force: territory, quotas, and compensation structure. I found a lot of wisdom in this statement. Although managing a financial advisory business is a bit different, the fact remains that the incentive *structure* of a professional relationship is the biggest determinant of its long-term success or failure.

### Commissions

The financial advisory industry was built on commissions. Somewhere along the way, "commission" became a dirty word. Some people even changed it to "transaction charge." Some good reasons exist for the negative connotation—four reasons actually.

### Four problems with a commission- or transaction-based relationship:

1. The advisor is incentivized to "sell" products and/or make changes in order to get paid.

2. The commission varies by product so there is a built-in conflict of interest.

3. It is much more profitable to sell new investments to new clients than it is to spend your time providing service to your existing clients.

4. Sometimes, the advisor should make a change but can't because the compensation structure gets in the way. For example, let's say the advisor sold you an "A" share mutual fund that paid him a 5% commission. Then something happens and he realizes there is a better fund or that market conditions have changed and the fund he sold you is no longer appropriate. He or she may feel he can't make a change so soon because it would call his 5% commission into question. It would seem even worse if he sold you a different fund that also charged a 5% commission (even if that were the appropriate investment).

Don't get us wrong. Tens of thousands of ethical commission-based financial advisors are out there. The structure can work. However, when many advisors realized that clients were not comfortable with the commission-based relationship, they transitioned to a "Fee-Only" arrangement.

## "Fee-Only" Advisors

Fee-Only advisors do not accept commissions. They charge a management fee, which is typically a percentage of the assets they manage. The fee typically ranges from 1-2%. The more money your advisor is managing, the lower the percentage. Most people would agree that this arrangement is superior for several reasons:

1. You never have to second guess why your advisor is recommending changes. Every time he buys or sell something,

it is just more work for him. Therefore, you can assume that he is only going to make changes if he thinks it will improve your situation.

2. No conflict of interest exists since your advisor gets paid the same amount regardless of which investments he uses.

3. Your advisor has the flexibility to buy and sell as often as necessary without the financial penalty of commissions.

4. The right incentives will motivate your advisor. He gets to charge his fee on a larger account when he makes you money. On the other hand, he takes a pay cut when your account declines in value. The other major incentive is to provide excellent service so you never want to leave. This is a win-win structure.

## "Fee-Based" Advisors

After reading the last two pages, you would assume that the authors of this book are "Fee-Only" advisors. We are not. We are a hybrid, known in the industry as "Fee-Based." Fee Based advisors have the flexibility to earn commissions *or* fees. Fee-Only sounds good to most consumers. The part they don't realize is that fees are not always best for the client. For example, some clients will need services that are truly a one-time transaction (e.g. purchasing long-term care insurance, term life insurance, a real estate transaction). It is not fair to the client to charge ongoing management fees if there is nothing actively to manage. Most Fee-Only advisors make a big deal of promoting the fact that they are Fee-Only. However, they frequently refer you to another advisor when you need a service for which they cannot charge their fee.

Fee-Based advisors must be dually licensed and subject to more regulatory oversight. This structure enables them to charge a fee for ongoing management of your investment portfolio, but they also have the flexibility to earn commissions for one-time transactions that fall outside of portfolio management. The most important thing is that your advisor should always disclose how he is being compensated and should earn either commissions or fees on a single transaction but not both. This structure allows the advisor to serve all the client's needs and employ the compensation method that is most fair for the services being offered.

### Don't Buy Investments, Buy Solutions

The financial services industry is continually evolving. Fewer and fewer "stock brokers" will call you up with an "idea" or a hot investment. However, it is still far too common for investors to be looking to their financial advisor to sell them one or two investments. It is even worse when prospective clients come in and say, "I am interested in an annuity" or "I want to buy a real estate investment trust (REIT)." Many problems can exist in these situations, which we explain further below:

1. Whenever a financial advisor is selling a single investment, the focus is always on past performance. Have you ever heard a financial advisor say, "This investment has done lousy lately, but it is going to come back"? Probably not, but that is the way investments work. You should buy when prices are down. The problem is that if the advisor has to sell you on a particular investment, he is going to sell what is hot because that is what people naturally want to buy. A good financial advisor protects

you from your instinct to chase whatever is hot, and doesn't buy into it himself.

2. Investments should not be viewed in isolation but as part of a portfolio. The exact amount that should be invested in any one thing should be based on the goal you are trying to achieve, your risk tolerance, family dynamics, income needs, etc. The allocations in the portfolios we manage for clients are planned down to the fraction of a percentage (e.g. commodities may be 7.3% of a portfolio). If someone is trying to sell you a single investment, it may not be part of your overall plan.

3. Typically, a single investment should be a small portion of your overall portfolio. In our practice, we constantly see people with too much money in too few investments. This imbalance results in unnecessary and uncompensated risk.

## Discretionary Accounts

Recently, we had a prospective client in our office who was trying to find a financial advisor to manage her retirement accounts. The meeting was going great until we explained that we are a "discretionary money manager." This term means we agree up front on your risk tolerance, income needs, and performance expectations, but then it is our job to make the daily investment decisions. In other words, we are not going to call each client in order to get his or her permission every time we want to buy or sell. Naturally, for portfolio management, we are not earning commissions on any trades, so we do not have any incentive to make changes unless we feel it will benefit the client.

This particular lady had a hard time accepting that we would be making changes without her input on each investment. It is important here to explain why we need discretion because most serious and successful money managers will have the same requirement. When you invest in a mutual fund, you have a fund manager (or managers) who manage that fund for thousands of people. They do their best to make prudent investment decisions based on many hours of research and on how each investment affects the fund as a whole. Do you really want that manager to call you to ask whether you think it's time to buy IBM? Wouldn't you be a little concerned about that? It is the same way when working with a discretionary money manager.

Markets move quickly and individual investments can move even faster. When we think it is time to sell a particular position, we frequently do not have the luxury of time to wait until we can call hundreds of clients to explain why we are selling this investment and why another investment is a better fit. Many money managers use dozens of investments and possibly even over a hundred different investments. It would be impossible to manage the portfolios if the money managers were spending all their time convincing each client why each trade was necessary. That being said, many discretionary money managers are able to accommodate specific requests such as: "Don't buy me any more AT&T or tobacco stocks," or "Don't ever sell a certain stock that has a large capital gain." Discretionary money managers are also usually happy to explain, after the fact, why they made specific decisions.

The protection you have when working with a discretionary money manager is that your money is typically liquid. This liquidity enables you to fire your money manager at any time if you are unhappy.

By comparison, a financial advisor who manages money on a non-discretionary basis (needs permission) typically uses far fewer investments, gets paid by commissions, and makes changes much less frequently.

## HOW TO MEASURE PERFORMANCE

The real question is: Is your financial advisor competent and doing a good job? His or her performance should not be measured strictly by raw returns and definitely not by short-term returns. What if your advisor gets great returns for a number of years and then loses half your money? You might have thought he was doing a great job, but really, he was getting lucky while taking too much risk.

This situation is like two people each driving to the same location. One driver speeds, weaves in and out of traffic, and runs the red lights. Luckily, he did not get into an accident or get a ticket. The other driver arrives five minutes later to find the first driver laughing and having a good time. The slower driver might feel like he was being too cautious especially if this happens every day. However, one day the reckless driver will not be so lucky and the price paid may be irreversible. Once an accident occurs, it will be apparent that arriving five minutes early was not worth the risk. Naturally, it is also possible to drive too slowly, which can also be dangerous.

The bottom line is that you have to consider both returns and risk when evaluating performance. Most people do not realize that risk can be measured. The most common measurements of risk are Standard Deviation and Beta. Imagine two investors who each earned the same return but one has half the risk. They may have earned the same return this year, but what happens in a bad year? In terms of our driving analogy, if you can get the same returns with less risk, it is like arriving every day at the same time as the reckless driver because you drove safely but took a more direct route.

A study published in January 2011 by a group of economics professors at the University of Kentucky, entitled "Do Investors Care about Risk? Evidence from Mutual Fund Flows" stated:

> We find clear evidence that investor inflows and outflows strongly chase past performance without regard to risk. In fact, the best performing funds are typically among the riskiest funds, so return chasing leads to apparent risk-seeking behavior. This behavior is particularly strong for retail investors....
>
> The fact that risk is immaterial to the average mutual fund investor creates interesting incentives for fund managers. A number of studies indicate that fund managers generally are unable to produce positive, risk-adjusted returns. This finding is often cited as proof that managers lack skill or that markets are efficient (or both). However, this conclusion begs the question of whether managers are incentivized to produce risk-adjusted returns in the first place.

## Compared to What?

Whether you think your returns are good or bad, the question is compared to what? Many people compare the return of their investment portfolio to a stock market index, like the S&P 500. This comparison is only viable if your portfolio is made up almost entirely of large cap U.S. stocks. However, it is a terrible comparison for most diversified portfolios. Large cap U.S. stocks may only make up

10-20% of a diversified portfolio these days. Therefore, it does not make sense to compare your returns to the S&P 500 or Dow Jones Industrial Index.

The entire purpose of diversification is to build a portfolio of investments that do not all go up or down at the same time. Therefore, your portfolio shouldn't consistently be tracking with one asset class. For example, if the S&P 500 is having a terrible year (e.g. 2008), then other investments in the portfolio should be helping you and enabling you to outperform the index. However, if the S&P is having a blockbuster year (e.g. 2009), then the other investments in your portfolio will be moderating your return. It's just like being a passenger on an airplane. You know where you want to go; now you want the pilot to get you there with as few bumps as possible. The goal of your money manager should also be to get you to your desired destination (goal) with as little volatility as possible. That means your boom years may not be as booming, but your disappointing years will not be as disappointing. That's good because, unlike your kids or grandkids, you probably don't like roller-coasters anymore.

The other problem with measuring performance based on an index is: What if the index has lousy returns for long periods of time? The S&P 500 has had virtually zero returns over the past 11 years. We are pretty sure that our clients would not be happy if we delivered zero return for a decade or even if we outperformed by returning 1 or 2%. Remember, you are not hiring a money manager to compete with an index. You are hiring him or her to secure your lifestyle and provide the income and assets you need to live the life you want to live. It is his job to figure out how best to accomplish that.

## Keep a Long-Term Perspective

Individual businesses and the overall economy go in cycles. These cycles include periods where business is terrible and the economy is contracting (i.e. in a recession). Then, the economy hits bottom (trough) and turns around (expansion). Eventually, the economy peaks and the cycle starts over. We have been through that process 33 times since 1854.[2] Naturally, the financial markets (stocks, bonds, real estate) rise and fall with the health of the economy. The business cycle has been getting longer in recent decades. In fact, the last three business cycles have been among the longest in history (average 8.8 years). Curiously, the average holding period for retail investors has been getting shorter. The average holding period for a retail mutual fund today is only 2.5-2.9 years (depending on which study you believe). Some well-known mutual funds and most individual stocks have average holding periods of only seven or eight months! In short, investors are not giving their investments enough time to work.

Jumping from one investment or even one money manager to another typically does not serve investors well. Consider a study that looked at 502 mutual funds whose performance was in the top quartile for the 10-year period that ended 12/31/2009. Although those funds had great 10-year numbers, 85% of those funds spent at least 3 out of 10 years underperforming their peers.[3]

Another research study conducted by investment consulting firm Cambridge Associates analyzed 92 retirement plans over a five-year

---

2    Source: National Bureau of Economic Research
3    Source: "The Next Chapter in the Active versus Passive Debate: an analysis of active management performance, persistency and efficacy." 2010 update. DiMeo Schneider & Associates, LLC.

period. Those plans removed 652 funds and added 907 others. The study found that the funds that were replaced underperformed their benchmarks by 1.7 percentage points over the three-year period prior to their replacement. However, those same funds ended up outpacing their benchmarks by 6.6 percentage points over the three-year period after replacement. In summary, the study found that the decision to switch funds, often on the basis of short-term criteria, usually led to destruction of value.

## So, When Should I Fire My Advisor?

Your financial advisor should design an investment plan to accomplish your specific goals. He or she should educate you on the range of potential returns (worst case, best case) and the expected average annual return over any rolling five-year period. We believe it is not prudent to judge performance over a timeframe of shorter than five years unless there are some glaring issues. Glaring issues would include:

- The advisor doesn't return your calls.

- Significant deviation in returns from your long-term plan over a five-year period or more.

- More volatility and risk than what was represented.

- Trading or moves that don't make sense and/or can't be explained when questioned.

Keep in mind that just because you plan to give a money manager five years doesn't mean that you shouldn't ask questions along the way. Let's suppose that your portfolio is up 5% for the year, but you think you should be doing better. So, you ask your financial advisor why the performance has not been better. Here are some examples of answers that do not inspire confidence and may lead you to question whether this advisor is right for you:

- We were trying to time the market and got it wrong.

- We made a big investment that didn't work out.

- We've been sitting on a lot of cash and we are trying to put it to work.

- Our strategy doesn't work well in this type of market.

Here is an answer that is more in line with what you want to hear:

- The U.S. stock market is up 9%. Our U.S. stocks are up that much or more. However, U.S. stocks only represent 25% of our portfolio. We also have a large allocation to emerging markets. This asset class has lagged this year. Unfortunately, it is virtually impossible to time short-term moves in these markets. It is a bit like surfing; when the wave comes, you have to be in the water and positioned to catch it. We strongly believe that emerging markets will be one of the leading asset classes over the next three to five years, and the valuations are very favorable right now. So we feel we are well-positioned, and we are sticking with our current allocation. We believe our clients will be rewarded for their patience.

## TWELVE QUESTIONS TO ASK WHEN CHOOSING A FINANCIAL ADVISOR

Finding the right financial advisor is very important. You should be prepared with a list of questions and have an idea of what you are looking for. Your questions should be detailed—after all, this is an interview. Don't just ask simple questions with predictable answers like, "Is this a good time to invest?" The answer to that is always going to be "Yes." Also, instead of asking an advisor what he is good at, ask what he is not good at. Here are some sample questions to get you started:

### 1. What experience do you have?

Find out how long the advisor has been in practice and the number and types of companies with which he or she has been associated. Ask the advisor what areas/topics are *not* his or her primary areas of expertise.

### 2. What are your qualifications?

The term "financial advisor" is used loosely by many financial professionals. Consumers may be shocked to find out how easy it is to get some designations. Some take as little as a week and it is hard to believe that advisors would actually put these designations on their business cards. So don't be afraid to ask probing questions. Ask the advisor what qualifies him to offer financial planning advice. The most relevant and respected designations are as a Certified Financial Planner (CFP®), a Certified Public Accountant-Personal Financial Specialist (CPA-PFS®), a Chartered Financial Consultant (ChFC®), a

Certified Investment Management Analyst (CIMA®), or a Chartered Financial Analyst (CFA®).

Keep in mind that each of these designations has its own specialties. Very few people are both great financial planners *and* investment analysts. Those are two different skill sets.

A good financial planner is going to help you:

- determine how much you need to save for retirement, or if you are retired, how much you can safely withdraw each year

- determine how your accounts should be titled and how beneficiaries should be listed

- coordinate estate and tax planning

- ensure proper insurance coverage

- when you need money, determine the best place to take it from

- make decisions about pensions, Social Security, and the best way to accomplish various financial goals

A good financial analyst or money manager is going to:

- research and select the specific stocks, bonds, mutual funds, limited partnerships and other investment vehicles

- manage the risk inside your investment portfolio based on current economic conditions and world events

Let's take the CIMA® and CFP® designations for example. These are the designations that the authors of this book have (Robert CIMA® and Jeremy CFP®). Before we merged our respective practices four years ago, Jeremy relied on other people to manage the money for his clients and Robert relied on other people to do the financial planning for his clients. Before the merger, at least we knew enough to outsource what we didn't know. Please beware of somebody who professes to be both a tremendous planner and money manager. Each skill set requires a different focus, different credentials, and many hours of continuing education to remain at the top of your field. It's better to have a team of specialists than one generalist who is mediocre at everything. In other words, you wouldn't want your podiatrist doing your bypass surgery.

### 3. What services do you offer?

The services a financial advisor can offer depend on a number of factors including credentials, licenses, and areas of expertise. It is important to know an advisor's limitations. If he is only licensed to sell insurance products, then that may clearly color his recommendations. Warren Buffett once said, "Never ask a barber if you need a haircut."

Ask the advisor, "What financial products are you *not* licensed to offer to your clients?"

### 4. Who is your "ideal" client?

Ask the financial advisor about the type of clients and situations with whom he typically likes to work. Make sure the advisor's viewpoint on investing is not too cautious or overly aggressive for you. Some advisors require you to have a certain net worth or minimum account size. Find out if the advisor will carry out the financial recommendations developed for you or refer you to someone else.

5. **Tell me about two clients who have fired you and why? Tell me about two clients you have decided not to work with anymore and why?**

This question is extremely important. Advisors want your business so they are going to try to put their best foot forward. You can learn a lot more from hearing about the relationships that did not work out.

6. **Will you be the only person working with me?**

The financial advisor may work with you him- or herself or have others in the office who assist him/her. You should meet everyone who will be working with you.

7. **How will I pay for your services?**

As part of your financial planning agreement, the financial advisor should clearly tell you how he/she will be compensated for the services to be provided.

8. **Please describe any potential conflicts of interest? Which, (if any) proprietary products do you use?**

Some business relationships could affect the advisor's professional judgment and inhibit him or her from acting in your best interest. In general, you want a financial advisor who is independent and free to work with the widest variety of products/investments. Ask the advisor to provide you with a description of his or her conflicts of interest in writing.

## 9. Have you ever been publicly disciplined for any unlawful or unethical actions in your professional career?

Several government and professional regulatory organizations, such as FINRA (formerly NASD) and your state insurance and securities departments, keep records on the disciplinary history of financial advisors. Ask what organizations the advisor is regulated by and contact these groups to conduct a background check. All Registered Investment Advisors must be able to provide you with a disclosure form called Form ADV Part II or the state equivalent of that form.

## 10. Can I have it in writing?

Ask the advisor to provide you with a written agreement that details the services that will be provided. Keep this document in your files for future reference.

## 11. Can we have lunch together?

This relationship is important, so invest the time. Sometimes you can get a much better feel for a person by spending time with him in a social setting. You can learn more about his values, family, personal accomplishments, and whether or not he is a person you like and trust.

## 12. Where is my money held and what type of statements do I get?

Everyone is concerned about whom he can really trust since the days of Bernie Madoff. It is easy to know you are not being scammed if you follow this simple advice: insist on a third party custodian like TD Ameritrade, Schwab, or Fidelity. Your assets should always be independently verified. On a daily basis, you should also be able to get online and view your account balances as well as any transactions your advisors have made. You should also insist on third party performance reporting where a company independent of your financial advisor's firm and the custodian should provide you with a quarterly consolidated report of how your account is performing.

The reason Bernie Madoff was able to get away with his Ponzi scheme for so long was because he was his own custodian and created his own statement and performance reports. There was no transparency and no checks and balances. You must take it upon yourself to insist on these. At bare minimum, you want a separate custodian.

# CHAPTER 9

# FINAL THOUGHTS

*"No matter how rich you become, how famous or how powerful,*
*when you die the size of your funeral will still*
*pretty much depend on the weather."*
— Michael Prichard

Congratulations on making it to the final (and shortest) chapter. This book most likely challenged some of your thoughts and beliefs about money and investing. We hope that our book will motivate you to make whatever changes are required to realize your financial goals. If you made it this far, there are likely one or more topics discussed in the book that you may have questions about or would like to understand better. If so, send us an email with your thoughts, questions, comments, or feedback to info@svwealth.com. Now... our Final Thoughts:

1. People will be much happier when they give up the idea that they can "out guess" their neighbor or the other 100 million investors. The one thing that is clear is that very few people (if any) can accurately predict the future. The winning strategy is not to guess right. It is to be prepared for the full spectrum

of potential events (good markets, bad markets, high interest rates, low interest rates, ranges of inflation, good health, bad health, disability, long life, short life). We challenge you to think through these scenarios and focus more on the potential consequences of your decisions.

2. Many of the ideas and information contained in this book may indicate that you need to make some changes to your current financial plans and practices. Let's face it, change is difficult. In fact, most people don't change just because they want to. They typically only make changes when they feel they need or are forced to. That is why most New Year's resolutions are not kept. For example, many people want to stop smoking, but they don't feel they need to until after they have a heart attack. People change when their need for change becomes stronger than their natural desire to remain comfortable with what they know. Unfortunately, 50% of heart attacks are fatal. So we encourage you to take action while you have the opportunity.

3. Your family will not remember, nor particularly care which mutual funds or annuities you purchased. However, they will remember your final words to them and the state in which you left your financial affairs. It is very easy to procrastinate and assume that you have plenty of time. Let's hope you do. Nevertheless, we challenge you to begin drafting your "what if" letter and financial inventory today. We have provided a sample "what if" letter in Chapter 5 and a sample financial inventory is provided in Appendix B to help you get started. Your financial advisor should also be able to help you with these.

4. Over the past five decades, American's per capita income (with inflation taken into account) has doubled. The number of homes with dishwashers, air conditioners, computers, and flat panel color TVs has skyrocketed. We have more convenience and luxuries than ever before in history. Yet, over the past five decades, there has been no measurable increase in happiness.

Money is the most efficient labor-saving device ever created, yet people have less time and are more stressed than ever. Financial strain is also the number one cause of divorce. Study after study shows that money does not translate into happiness. Those same studies show that what consistently translates into happiness is close relationships with friends and family, a sense of community, and an activity (job or hobby) that gives you a sense of purpose. Many people lose sight of the fact that money should not be the goal. It is a natural human instinct (amplified by the media) always to want more. Our society celebrates wealth and celebrity, and we judge our own economic well-being by comparing ourselves to others. As Little Richard once said, "The grass may look greener on the other side, but believe me, it's just as hard to cut."

We work with a lot of wealthy people, and the one thing we have learned is that the highest and best use of money is as a tool that enables you to live a life you love. We encourage you to build your financial life in such a way that it reduces stress and enables you to spend the rest of your days enjoying hobbies, travel, and quality time with the people you love.

We hope this book has been helpful. Thanks for reading.

# DISCLOSURE

---

# RECOMMENDED READING

Ariely, Dan. *Predictably Irrational: The Hidden Forces That Shape Our Decisions.* Revised and expanded ed. New York: HarperPerennial, 2010.

Faber, Mebane T. and Eric W. Richardson. *The Ivy Portfolio: How to Invest Like the Top Endowments and Avoid Bear Markets.* Hoboken, NJ: John Wiley & Sons, 2009.

Klein, Gary. *Sources of Power: How People Make Decisions.* Cambridge, MA: MIT Press, 1999.

Lucia, Ray. *The Buckets of Money Retirement Solution: The Ultimate Guide to Income for Life.* Hoboken, NJ: John Wiley & Sons, 2010.

McKinsey & Company, Tim Koller, Marc Goedhart, and David Wessels. *Valuation: Measuring and Managing the Value of Companies.* 5th ed. Hoboken, NJ: John Wiley & Sons, 2010.

Montier, James. *The Little Book of Behavioral Investing: How Not to Be Your Own Worst Enemy.* Hoboken, NJ: John Wiley & Sons, 2010.

Nofsinger, John. *The Psychology of Investing.* 4th ed. Upper Saddle River, NJ: Prentice-Hall, 2010.

Swensen, David. *Pioneering Portfolio Management: An Unconventional Approach to Institutional Investment.* Revised ed. New York: Free Press, 2009.

# APPENDIX A

# ALTERNATIVE ASSET CLASS DEFINITIONS

**Absolute Return:** Absolute Return is any investment strategy designed to generate positive returns over a three to five year period, irrespective of the direction of stock or bond markets. This return is typically achieved by investing the portfolio's assets in cash or other low volatility investments and then taking hedged long and short positions in portfolios of securities, which when combined, are expected to have modest exposures to market returns. The resulting portfolio should have low correlation with financial market performance. Of course, whether such a portfolio actually delivers a positive absolute return depends on the skill of the portfolio manager in selecting profitable long and short positions.

**Arbitrage:** Attempting to profit by exploiting price differences of identical or similar financial instruments on different markets or in different forms. The ideal version is riskless arbitrage.

**Commodities:** Any unprocessed or partially processed good, which is typically used as a raw material to be processed and resold, such as petroleum, wheat, or copper. Its price is determined by supply and demand in a global market. There is no product differentiation among different producers.

**Currencies:** Buying or selling the currencies of different countries in order to profit on trends in the relative strength of one currency vs. another. Currencies can also be used to hedge other exposure (i.e. buying the U.S. dollar to hedge commodities priced in dollars).

**Emerging Market Debt:** Government bonds issued by the governments of countries known as emerging economies such as Brazil, India, and China.

**Hedged Equity:** Ownership of stock in publicly traded companies, which is then insured against declines in the value of the stock by using options contracts. A put option, for example, gives you the right to sell your stock at a pre-determined price (the strike price) and any time prior to the option's expiration date.

**Managed Futures:** The active trading of "Futures contracts," which are contracts to buy or sell an asset (stock index, commodity, currency, fixed income, or other security) for delivery at a specified future date at a specified price. Managed Futures are similar to stock options except that they are applied to assets other than stocks. Traders usually employ quantitative or technical analysis and systematic investment processes, which are designed to profit on price trends. The traders can profit regardless of whether the price trend of the underlying asset is up or down.

**Private Equity:** Ownership (i.e. stock) in operating companies that are not publicly traded.

**Real Estate:** Both domestic and international commercial real estate (office, industrial, multi-family, specialty).

# APPENDIX B

# FINANCIAL INVENTORY

---

THE SAMPLE FAMILY
PERSONAL FINANCIAL INVENTORY
SEPTEMBER 30, 2011

## INVESTMENTS

| Account Name | Institution | Account # | Value | Notes |
|---|---|---|---|---|
| Trust Account | TD Ameritrade | 012345434 | $680,312 | All TD Ameritrade accounts managed by Jeremy Kisner (480)555-5555, TDA (800)-555-5555, view accounts online at www.advisorclient.com, UN: samiam PW: whoissam |
| Sam SEP IRA | TD Ameritrade | 012345435 | $516,780 | |
| Sam ROTH IRA | TD Ameritrade | 012345432 | $63,692 | |
| Mary ROTH IRA | TD Ameritrade | 012345433 | $84,590 | |
| Penn Mutual Annuity (Non-Qualified) | Penn Mutual | 012345436 | $270,000 | Pays monthly income for Sam and Mary's life, death benefit (if any) to kids. View account online at www. pennmutual.com, UN: Samiam PW: whoissam (800)555-5555 |

## INVESTMENTS

| Account Name | Institution | Account # | Value | Notes |
|---|---|---|---|---|
| Jackson National Life Insurance (Sam) | Jackson National | 012345437 | $183,703 | Death Benefit $420,863 (grows with cash value). (800)555-5555, Premium paid quarterly $3k due in Jan, April, July, Oct |
| Capital One Savings Account (Joint owners) | Capital One | Acct, AAABBBCC Routing DDDEEFFFF | $35,000 | This is an emergency fund, fully liquid. Customer Svc (866)555-5555, www. capitalonedirect.com UN: Samsample, PW: Susie07, linked to Wells Fargo Checking Acct 5554321 |
| 529 Plan Tyler | American Funds | 012345432 | $44,654 | Set up through Jeremy Kisner, American Funds phone (800) 555 -5555 |
| 529 Plan Brooke | American Funds | 012345431 | $35,028 | |
| | Total Investable Assets | | $1,913,759 | |

NOTE: Primary Residence and Rental property are only major assets not included on this inventory of Investible Assets. They are listed on the Real Estate Inventory (next page)

## REAL ESTATE

| Property Description | Estimated Value | Mortgage Balance | Mortgage Servicer | Notes: |
|---|---|---|---|---|
| Primary Residence: 1234 Main Street, Las Vegas NV 89012 | $900,000 | $215,000 | Mortgage Servicer is IndyMac, P.O. Box 78826, Phoenix AZ 85062-8826, Loan #12345432, Phone (800)555-5555 | Fixed Rate mortgage @ 5.0%, Home will be paid off 4/2024. |
| | | $32,000 | HELOC: Wells Fargo, P.O. Box 688923 Des Moines IA 50368-8923, Account #12345678-1, Phone (800)555-5555 | Current rate is 4.0%, Prime +.25%, monthly payments made by linked checking account. |

## REAL ESTATE

| Property Description | Estimated Value | Mortgage Balance | Mortgage Servicer | Notes: |
|---|---|---|---|---|
| Rental Property: 238 Court Street, Henderson NV 89074 | $425,000 | $138,000 | Mortgage servicer is Nationstar Mtg, P.O. Box 650783, Dallas TX 75265-0783, Loan #01345432, Phone (888)555-5555 | Loan is adjustable. Next adjustment 8/2012. Current rate is 4.125%, currently paying down $810 per month of principal, break even cash flow on rental. Tenant on month-to-month lease. Owned by trust. Deed is in trust binder. Local property manager is Gary Smith (702)555-5555 at Broker's Realty. |
| Total Real Estate | $1,325,000 | $385,000 | | |
| Total Equity | $940,000 | | | |

NOTE: Both properties are owned by our revocable living trust.

## INSURANCE

| Account | Company | Amount of Coverage | Account Number | Notes |
|---|---|---|---|---|
| Long Term Care | John Hancock | $250 / day, 4 yrs coverage, 90 day elimination period. | L12345432 | Premium is $4,400 yr due in February, Phone (888)555-5555 |
| Permanent Life Insurance - Sam | Jackson National Life Ins Co. | 4204204 | 12345432 | Death Benefit $420,863 (increases with cash value). (800)555-5555, Premium paid quarterly $3k due in Jan, April, July, Oct |
| Homeowners - Rental | Liberty Mutual | $380,000 fire, $345,000 special form, $20,000 broad form | FN2-222-0000-1001 | All property / casualty insurance is with Liberty Mutual. Phone (702)555-5555, Agent is Mr. Insurance Agent. For Claims call (800)555-5555 |
| Home Owners - Primary Residence | Liberty Mutual | dwelling $731,000, PP $448, $1,000 deductible | H32-0000-306271 | |

## INSURANCE

| Account | Company | Amount of Coverage | Account Number | Notes |
|---|---|---|---|---|
| Umbrella Liability | Liberty Mutual | $1,000,000 | LJ1-555-000000-107 2 | |
| Auto | Liberty Mutual | $250 / $500, $1,000 deductible | A02-444-30000 | |

## BANKING

| Institution | Account Type | Account # | Approx Balance | Notes |
|---|---|---|---|---|
| Wells Fargo | Checking | 123454321 | $14,000 | Everyday checking account, over draft Line $2,500. Pay bills online from this account; mortgage comes out automatically on the 1st. Contact at bank is manager, Jerry Sips. Branch phone (702) 555-5555. Online access www.wellsfargo.com, UN: samiam PW: iamsam |
| Wells Fargo | Home Equity Line | 12345678-1 | $0 | $200k available. Zero current balance. Monthly payment (if any) made automatically from main Wells Fargo checking account. Interest rate is currently 4%. |

## BANKING

| Institution | Account Type | Account # | Approx Balance | Notes |
|---|---|---|---|---|
| Chase | Checking | 98765432 | $6,200 | Rental Real Estate Account, direct pay mortgage, DD of rental income by property manager (Gary Smith @ Broker's Realty). Main contact at Chase is Margaret Jones. Branch phone (702) 555-5555. Access accounts www.chase.com, UN: samiam PW: iamsam |
| Chase | CD | 24681357 | $50,000 | 5 yr CD @ 4.5% interest. Matures, 3/07/2014 |

NOTE: All bank documents are in 2nd drawer of file cabinet in Den. Penalty to cash in Chase CD if ever needed is 60 days interest.

## CONTACTS

| Person | Role | Contact Info |
|---|---|---|
| Rick Garrett | CPA | (702) 555-5555 office, (702)555-5555 cell<br>Street Address, City, State, ZIP |
| Richard Chatwin | Estate Planning Attorney | (702) 555-5555 office, (702)555-5555 cell<br>Street Address, City, State, ZIP |
| Jeremy Kisner | Financial Advisor | (702) 555-5555 office, (702)555-5555 cell<br>Street Address, City, State, ZIP |
| Hayden Ray | Insurance Agent (Property Casualty) | (702) 555-5555 office, (702)555-5555 cell<br>Street Address, City, State, ZIP |
| Rick Manheim | Funeral Director | (702) 555-5555 office, (702)555-5555 cell<br>Street Address, City, State, ZIP |
| Gary Smith | Property Manager | (702) 555-5555 office, (702)555-5555 cell<br>Street Address, City, State, ZIP |

# ABOUT SUREVEST CAPITAL MANAGEMENT

**SureVest Capital Management was founded in 2002 by Robert Luna.** Mr. Luna's goal was to bring his experience as a risk analyst and money manager for institutions and pension funds to individual investors. He noticed that many individual investors were getting confusing, conflicting, and often dangerous investment advice. Several financial advisors were also leading their clients into the most common investment traps such as chasing whatever is hot at the moment, making decisions based on emotion, trying to time markets, and managing retirement income portfolios the same way they managed accumulation portfolios. In short, people were paying for bad advice.

**In 2008, SureVest merged with Kisner & Associates,** a Las Vegas financial planning and wealth management firm. The combination brought a wealth of knowledge and resources in the areas of financial planning, tax planning, and estate planning.

**SureVest is an Independent Registered Investment Advisor,** meaning it is not biased by any in-house or proprietary products. Therefore, its staff is free to work objectively with the widest variety of investments. SureVest's mission is to build and protect wealth so people can live extraordinary lives. SureVest is able to deliver a level of service and performance that goes far beyond what people can expect from a traditional brokerage house relationship. It serves a distinct customer base, and for the benefit of its existing clients, only accepts a limited number of new clients each year. SureVest has offices in Phoenix and Las Vegas, but it serves clients nationwide.

Selecting the "right" wealth management firm is a difficult decision. No one firm can be right for everybody. SureVest strives to be the best choice for mid to high net worth individuals and families with a long-term financial perspective, who are seeking a competent trusted advisor.

Clients have told Robert and Jeremy, the respective CEO and President of SureVest, that what sets them and their company apart from other firms in the field are:

- A proactive approach to portfolio management.

- An ability to simplify complex financial decisions.

- A genuine interest in educating our clients and making sure they understand what we are doing for them and why.

# ABOUT THE AUTHORS

**Robert J. Luna, CIMA® and CEO/Chief Investment Officer of SureVest Capital Management**

Robert is a University of Pennsylvania, Wharton School of Business Alumnus. He graduated from Wharton's prestigious Advanced Management Program and was honored to become a Wharton Fellow in 2011, thereby joining an elite community who has made a lifelong commitment to learning. Robert also earned the professional designation of Certified Investment Management Analyst (CIMA®) at Wharton.

He holds the FINRA series 7, 4, 24, 65, and 63 licenses and has also completed advanced courses in risk management, financial planning, and modern portfolio theory through the College of Financial Planning. Robert has over 14 years of experience in managing assets for institutions, professional athletes, small business owners, and high net worth investors.

Prior to founding SureVest Capital Management in 2002, Robert held positions as a derivatives trader and risk analyst for a Wall Street firm and as a proprietary trader and Chief Risk Officer for a regional firm. He has been a regular speaker on financial talk radio KFNN in Phoenix & KNUU in Las Vegas. In addition, Robert has served as a contributing editor to various financial media sources.

Above all, Robert's passion for education, research, and strategy guides SureVest's mission to protect and grow its clients' wealth so they and their families can live extraordinary lives. Robert lives in Scottsdale, Arizona with wife Mia and daughter Bella.

### Jeremy A. Kisner, CFP®, CRPS®, and President of SureVest Capital Management

Jeremy is a Certified Financial Planner, Chartered Retirement Plans Specialist, and Certified Estate Planner. He has a degree in Economics from the University of California, Santa Barbara and has received advanced education in risk management, financial planning, and modern portfolio theory through the financial planning program at the University of California, Irvine. He holds the FINRA Series 7, 24, & 63 licenses as well as fixed and variable insurance licenses.

During 2008-2009, Jeremy was the host of the weekly financial talk radio show *Kisner's School of Money* on 970 AM KNUU in Las Vegas. His articles have also been published in various financial trade publications. Jeremy founded Kisner & Associates, a financial planning and wealth management firm in 2003, which merged with SureVest Capital in 2008.

Throughout his career, Jeremy has helped hundreds of individuals, business owners, and families. His particular areas of expertise include: retirement plan selection/design/implementation, retirement plan rollovers, income/distribution planning, alternative investments and asset protection. Jeremy lives in Las Vegas with his wife Angela and daughters Chloe, Gracie, and Maya.

**Jeremy describes his and Robert's relationship and collaboration at SureVest as follows:**

In January of 2007, I met Robert at our Broker Dealer's annual top producers conference. We were both already successful in the business and neither of us ever envisioned having a partner. However, while talking over dinner one night at the conference, I quickly realized two things: 1) I like this guy, and 2) he is a more sophisticated money manager than any of the other reps at the conference (including me). I was trying to pick Robert's brain regarding how he manages money, and he was very forthcoming with ideas and information. I decided to push my luck and ask whether I could come to Scottsdale to see his operation, the software he used, etc. He said, "Sure," so I went. He was very helpful and we kept in touch after that.

At the next conference, we sat together the entire conference and it quickly became apparent that we had different skill sets but the same values. We decided to try working together. We started with baby steps. I registered as an Investment Advisor Representative of his company, SureVest. I brought on a few new clients for whom I did the financial planning and Robert managed the client's investments. At first, we kept our company names and operations separate. Over time, however, the relationship and service offerings became more cohesive. In late 2008, we decide to merge our firms. It seemed logical to keep the SureVest name since it was generic, as opposed to my firm's name: Kisner & Associates.

Since then, the business has grown tremendously, and we are truly offering a better client experience than either of us could have delivered on our own. We honestly have never had a disagreement and both try to err on the side of generosity in all of our business dealings. In addition to being business partners, we are great friends.

For more information about Robert Luna, Jeremy Kisner, and SureVest, visit:

**WWW.SVWEALTH.COM**

# NOTES